S•T•R•E•
H WISE C
OUR DOLLARS
ANAGEMENT

ALSO BY DAVID L. SCOTT

The Guide to Personal Budgeting (Money Smarts)

The Guide to Investing in Bonds (Money Smarts)

The Guide to Investing in Common Stocks (Money Smarts)

The Guide to Investing in Mutual Funds (Money Smarts)

The Guide to Buying Insurance (Money Smarts)

Understanding and Managing Investment Risk and Return

Dictionary of Accounting

Fundamentals of the Time Value of Money

The Investor's Guide to Discount Brokers

Stretching Your Income:
101 Ways to Help You Cope with Inflation

Security Investments

Finance

Wall Street Words

Investing in Tax-Saving Municipal Bonds

Municipal Bonds: The Basics and Beyond

by David L. Scott

OLD SAYBROOK, CONNECTICUT

This book's purpose is to provide accurate and authoritative information on the topics covered. It is sold with the understanding that neither the author nor the publisher is rendering legal, financial, accounting, or other professional services. Neither the Globe Pequot Press nor the author assumes any liability resulting from action taken based on the information included herein. Mention of a company name does not constitute endorsement.

Library of Congress Cataloging-in-Publication Data

Scott, David Logan, 1942–
The guide to managing credit / David L. Scott. — 1st ed.
p. cm. — (Money smarts)
Includes index.
ISBN 1-56440-472-2
1. Consumer credit—United States. I. Title. II. Series: Scott, David Logan, 1942– Money smarts
HG3756.U54S38 1994
332.7'43—dc20 94-12139
CIP

Manufactured in the United States of America
First Edition/First Printing

Contents

About the Author

David L. Scott is professor of accounting and finance at Valdosta State College, Valdosta, Georgia. Professor Scott was born in Rushville, Indiana, and received degrees from Purdue University and Florida State University before earning a Ph.D. in economics from the University of Arkansas at Fayetteville.

David has written more than twenty books, including *Wall Street Words* for Houghton Mifflin and *The Guide to Personal Budgeting*, *The Guide to Investing in Common Stocks*, *The Guide to Investing in Bonds*, *The Guide to Investing in Mutual Funds*, and *The Guide to Buying Insurance* in this series. He and his wife, Kay, are the authors of the two-volume *Guide to the National Park Areas* for the Globe Pequot Press. David and Kay spend their summers traveling throughout the United States and Canada in their fourth Volkswagen Camper.

Introduction

With sufficient wealth you won't have to worry about learning to manage credit, because you won't need to borrow any money. Some people are in this situation, but not many, and probably not you. Many families struggle with debt that is continuously rolled forward, month after month, year after year. Hopefully, you aren't in this situation either. Credit, if abused, can ruin the quality of your life just as surely as bad health or a bad marriage. In fact, persistent credit difficulties can often end up causing health and marriage problems.

It is possible to gain control of your borrowing, even if you have been a chronic credit abuser. The cure isn't easy, and it certainly isn't painless. Most people who end up with credit difficulties do so because they are unable to control their impulse to spend. You are going to experience credit difficulties no matter how much income you earn if you can't rein in your spending. Understanding where and how to shop for credit is important, of course, because it allows you to save on finance charges. But saving some finance charges is going to be like spitting in the wind if you owe so much money you have to take out additional loans just to keep current on your existing debt.

There are no magic solutions in this book. If your debt is increasing toward the point where you will have difficulty making the required payments to creditors, there is little advice to offer other than to cut back on the money you spend. On a more pleasant note, you will find some tips and ideas that you may be able to put to use. Chapter 3 includes a discussion of how interest rates are calculated. If you think there is only one way to calculate interest rates, you had better read this section of the book carefully. Two lenders can quote the same interest rate on the same transaction and still end up hitting you with different interest charges. Is this a confusing world, or what?

After reading this book you should have a better understanding of

- how interest rates are affected by the level of economic activity;
- how government policy affects the interest rates you pay;
- which lenders you should contact for specific types of loans;
- how to compare interest rate quotations from different lenders;
- how credit card companies can quote the same interest rate and yet assess widely varying finance charges;
- the best way to prepare when you will be seeking a loan;
- how to determine your credit limit; and
- the importance of a personal budget in managing your credit.

A big part of debt management is nothing more than applying common sense to financial matters. If you are currently experiencing difficulties making ends meet, it should be fairly obvious that buying a new car is likely to send you over the edge. Still, many consumers finance purchases of things they don't really need even though they can barely make the payments on their current debt. Sound familiar? Read on.

David L. Scott
Valdosta, Georgia

CHAPTER 1

An Overview of Credit

Buying on credit has become a way of life for most individuals, families, businesses, and governments. There are valid reasons to borrow; at the same time, indiscriminate and excessive credit use can cause financial difficulties for both borrowers and creditors. Finance charges that result from credit use make goods and services more expensive for a borrower. Credit availability and credit use have a major impact on a country's economic activity.

Borrowing involves obtaining money, goods, or services in return for a promise of future repayment. Loans can originate with the supplier of a good or service (e.g., a business that sells you something on credit) or with a third party (e.g., a bank or credit union). Borrowing results from a decision to buy now and pay later. Rather than purchase a good or service a little at a time (e.g., buy one piece of furniture at a time) or save until sufficient funds are available to pay in full, borrowing allows you to acquire and enjoy a good or service in return for agreeing to make a future payment or series of payments.

The availability and use of credit have a major impact on the domestic and international economy. Increased credit availability and accompanying reductions in interest rates influence businesses and individuals to increase their borrowing and spending. Lower interest rates stimulate home building, automobile sales (to a lesser extent), and business spending for plant and equipment, all of which cause businesses to expand output and hire more workers in an attempt to increase profits.

Federal authorities regularly take steps to influence credit availability in an attempt to affect economic activity. Authorities concerned about high or rising unemployment, reduced business investment spending, and deteriorating economic activity work to increase the availability of credit, especially prior to an upcoming election. Policies are implemented to restrict credit growth when the economy is operating near full capacity and inflation is a concern. Restricted credit availability and the accompanying increase in interest rates have a negative influence on lending and economic activity.

The Good and Bad of Credit Use and Abuse

Buying on credit isn't financially unsound or ethically wrong so long as you don't borrow to excess and you don't squander money on unneeded goods and services that you would ordinarily forgo. The availability of credit has become an important consideration in many large purchases. Most families would be unable to enjoy a home of their own if all real estate purchases were made only for cash. Businesses routinely use borrowed funds to help pay for inventories, new equipment, and factories, and to provide financing for acquisitions and internal modifications that increase their efficiency and competitiveness. Businesses would find it difficult to grow and compete if credit was unavailable.

Borrowers' need for funds benefits individuals and companies that have excess funds. These savers are provided with an opportunity to earn investment income on cash that would otherwise remain idle. Excess funds sometimes find their way directly to borrowers. Businesses that have extra funds often lend money to other businesses that are in need of money. Likewise, individual investors funnel money to businesses and governments by purchasing newly issued debt securities. Individuals ordinarily make their extra monies accessible to borrowers by depositing the funds in financial intermediaries (e.g., banks, credit unions, and savings & loan associations) that, in turn, lend the funds to families and businesses needing additional monies. The bottom line is that credit availability sustains a great many businesses and jobs at the same time that it makes life more pleasant for individuals and families who have the financial discipline to intelligently use this source of money.

On the negative side, interest charges on borrowed funds have the effect of increasing the cost of goods and services that are purchased on credit. Individuals, businesses, and governments sometimes borrow to excess, especially when credit is readily available. Excessive use of credit can cause a borrower to incur such large financial obligations that little money is available for normal spending needs. Unrestrained borrowing has been a cause of stress, broken marriages, bankrupt companies, and governments unable to pay for essential services.

Potential Advantages of Credit Use

1. *Credit allows you to readily acquire and enjoy the use of expensive items.* A large amount of borrowing is used to purchase assets that provide years of use or enjoyment. Purchasing a new automobile with borrowed money permits you to enjoy ownership of the vehicle while you repay the loan. When the loan is repaid in three or four years you will own the car free and clear of debt. Depending on the vehicle's condition and your own desire for a newer model, you will be ready to drive the car a few more years or trade it for something newer. The routine will then begin yet again. Without the availability of credit, you would have to save for many months or years in order to be able to acquire expensive items.
2. *Credit provides you with an emergency source of funds.* What would you do if your car broke down and, because you didn't have sufficient funds to pay for the required repairs, left you stranded in a distant town? What would you do if your home's furnace gave out during the winter and you were short of savings to pay for a re-

placement? Nearly everyone encounters situations in which insufficient money is available to take care of some pressing need. Credit provides you with the ability to obtain, on relatively short notice, the money that is required to bridge a temporary shortage of funds.

3. *Borrowing can produce tax savings.* Interest paid on certain types of loans can be deducted in calculating your taxable income and the resulting income tax liability. Individual taxpayers are permitted to deduct the interest paid on loans used to buy first and second homes (motor homes and boats sometimes also qualify), and interest charges on borrowing used to acquire certain income-producing investments are generally deductible in calculating income taxes. Interest paid by individuals on most consumer loans and credit card balances is not permitted as a tax deduction. Businesses are permitted to deduct nearly all their interest expenses in calculating their income tax liabilities.
4. *Credit allows you to make a purchase prior to a price increase.* You may have decided to purchase something that you anticipate will soon increase in price. Perhaps you have been thinking about buying a house, jewelry, fuel oil, wallpaper, or a million other things. Rather than wait until you are able to accumulate sufficient funds to make the purchase at the higher price, credit availability permits you to use borrowed money to make the purchase prior to the price increase. For example, you may have read in the paper that there will soon be a $700 increase in the price of an automobile you have been planning to purchase. You may be better off buying now, at the lower price, even though the earlier purchase will cause you to have to borrow a portion of the current

purchase price. Being able to acquire a product before its price increases is especially beneficial during periods of high inflation.

5. *Credit availability provides convenience.* It is frequently convenient to pay for a good or service by using a credit source rather than by paying with cash. Ordering by telephone nearly always requires that you have access to a credit card. The alternative of sending a check may cause you to wait weeks until the seller is satisfied that your check is good. Credit cards are virtually mandatory for certain transactions, such as renting a vehicle. Owning a credit card also allows you to guarantee hotel room reservations without being required to submit a check as a deposit.
6. *Certain credit sources permit you to pay later without being charged interest.* Being able to delay the payment for a good or service without being charged a fee is to your advantage because it allows you to retain control over your money for a longer period of time. Credit card issuers often allow users up to thirty days to pay for a purchase without incurring any fees or interest charges. Some retailers, especially furniture companies, offer customers the opportunity to make delayed payments without incurring interest charges. So long as you aren't charged any interest or fees, it is to your advantage to put off paying for a purchase as long as possible.
7. *Credit allows you to travel or shop without being required to carry large amounts of cash.* Keeping large amounts of cash in your possession subjects you to the risk that the money will be lost or stolen. Carrying cash also makes it more likely that you will be subject to a mugging. Traveler's checks are an alternative to cash or

credit cards but they are sometimes inconvenient to buy and their purchase may entail a fee. Carrying cash or travelers checks (as opposed to a credit card) keeps you from earning interest on these funds. Buying $2,000 in traveler's checks means you have $2,000 less money that is invested and producing income.

8. *Buying on credit allows you to use someone else's money while you retain control over your own funds.* Credit allows you to acquire goods and services without being required to use your own funds. Perhaps your funds are profitably invested and yet you need to purchase some new clothing or trade cars. Borrowing makes it possible to acquire whatever it is that you need at the same time your funds remain fully invested. This is an advantage only when you are able to earn a return that is higher than the rate you are paying a creditor.
9. *Lenders sometimes offer borrowers special benefits at no additional cost.* Competition among creditors, especially issuers of credit cards, has caused lenders to offer customers a variety of freebies. Credit card issuers often provide cardholders with frequent flier points (1 point per dollar charged), insurance on damage of rental cars, warranty extensions on goods purchased, specialized life insurance coverage, and so forth. These perks are generally available without charge on certain cards.

Don't pay extra for a gold card, a platinum card, or a plutonium card if you won't utilize the features of these cards. You must not have much self-esteem if you feel you have to impress your associates with the color of your credit card.

10. *Paying by credit card creates a helpful spending record* The detailed spending record provided by monthly credit card statements is particularly valuable for someone who maintains a personal budget. Some credit card issuers provide a year-end statement with charges grouped into spending categories.
11. *Credit purchases often provide leverage in the event a problem develops with your purchase.* When you pay cash for a purchase, you often have little clout if something goes wrong with your purchase. Once a business has your money it may have little reason to make certain you are satisfied with your purchase. On the other hand, owing money to a merchant who fears you might not pay places you in a better position to push for a satisfactory solution to your problem.

Potential Disadvantages of Credit Use

1. *Credit availability makes it easy to buy goods and services that ordinarily would not be purchased.* Credit provides increased buying power that many individuals, families, and institutions find difficult to hold in check. Goods and services that would ordinarily remain unpurchased are bought and consumed when sufficient credit is available. Paying cash makes it clear that buying one thing precludes you from buying something else. Being

> There are several acceptable methods for calculating finance charges on a credit card balance. Make certain you choose a credit card from an issuer that uses a method most favorable to you.

Figure 1

INCREASED COST OF USING CREDIT
COMPARED WITH PAYING CASH

Cash Price	Interest Rate on Loan	Payment Frequency	Payment Amount	Number of Payments	Total of Payments	Increased Cost
$10,000	6%	annual	$10,600	1	$ 10,600	$ 600
12,000	8	monthly	376	36	13,536	1,536
12,000	8	monthly	243	60	14,580	2,580
500	12	monthly	44	12	528	28
95,000	7	monthly	632	360	227,520	132,520
95,000	10	monthly	834	360	300,240	205,240
95,000	7	monthly	854	180	153,720	58,720
3,000	9	monthly	137	24	3,288	288

able to pay for purchases with borrowed money short circuits the financial discipline that is imposed by cash purchases.

2. *Borrowing generally increases the cost of acquiring a good or service.* Fees and interest that are charged by lenders result in a higher cost for goods and services that are purchased with borrowed money. The sum of all the payments you make on an automobile loan might amount to $18,000 when you could have purchased the vehicle for a cash price of $14,500. The higher the interest rate and the longer a loan's term, the more that credit adds to the cost of a purchase. Lenders frequently impose fees for originating a loan, paying late, and repaying a loan prior to the scheduled maturity.

The examples in Figure 1 illustrate the additional cost that a consumer must pay when credit is used to pay for the purchase of goods and services. The $12,000 loan that is shown might represent borrowing for an automobile, while the larger, $95,000 loan might represent a loan to purchase a home. Other, smaller loans could be for a home improvement project or a vacation. Notice that the additional cost of buying on credit is influenced by both the length of time before the loan is scheduled to be repaid and the rate of interest that is charged. For example, an 8 percent five-year car loan (sixty months) will cause you to pay in excess of $1,000 more in interest compared with a three-year loan for the same amount and at the same interest rate. As you would expect, payments are substantially higher for the shorter loan ($376 vs. $243). The three alternative payment schedules for the $95,000 home loan produce even wider cost variations. Borrowing $95,000 for thirty years at a 7 percent interest rate will cause you to pay total interest charges of $132,520 even though the $632 payments gradually reduce the balance on the loan. Repaying the loan in fifteen years requires a higher monthly payment of $854 but saves nearly $75,000 in total interest ($58,720 vs. $132,520). The same loan at 10 percent interest requires monthly payments of $834 and results in total credit costs of $205,240 over the thirty-year life of the loan.

3. *Credit availability results in many individuals and businesses becoming mired in debt.* Individuals and busi-

> Interest rates on unpaid credit card balances are relatively high compared with the rates of most other sources of credit. It is important that you not run up large balances on your card.

nesses sometimes borrow such a large amount of money that they are unable to remain current on their loan obligations. Personal and corporate bankruptcies increased dramatically in the 1980s and 1990s as borrowers sought to escape their financial obligations. More than a few marriages have collapsed from financial problems caused by credit abuse.

4. *Frequent credit use allows lenders to monitor your spending habits.* The more purchases you charge, the more data about your spending activities creditors and merchants are able to accumulate. Cash payments for goods and services don't produce a trail that allows others to learn how you have been spending your money.

Don't assume that just because the advantages section is longer, borrowing is the preferred method of paying for goods and services. Borrowing has the potential to cause severe financial problems that can wreck someone's life. Individuals without the discipline to control borrowing are better off avoiding credit use altogether (other than for the purchase of a home).

Why Borrow?

Individuals, businesses, and governments borrow for several reasons. Most important by far is the fact that individuals and organizations frequently don't have sufficient funds to pay in full for purchases they are unable or unwilling to put off. Some purchases entail a substantial expense that would normally be impossible without using borrowed money. Individuals borrow to buy homes, businesses borrow to buy factories, and governments borrow to build highways. Bor-

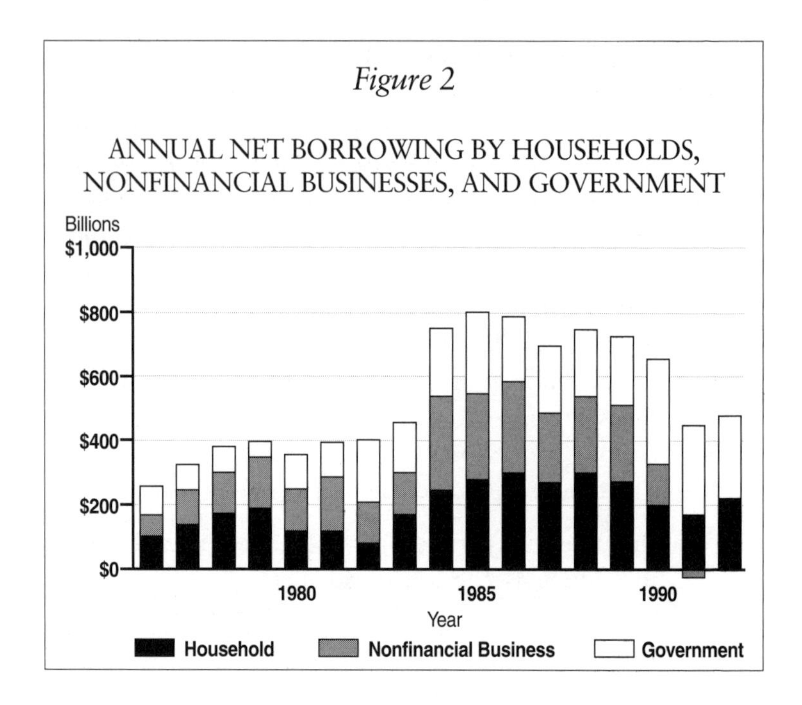

rowers sometimes make a decision to avoid dipping into their savings even though sufficient funds are available to pay in full for their purchases. For example, a family with substantial savings may decide to borrow most of the purchase price of a new automobile.

Business Borrowing. Businesses are typically financed with a combination of borrowed money, ownership contributions, and funds that have been retained from profits. Borrowing provides businesses with an alternative source of capital to purchase additional productive assets (e.g., machinery and buildings) and to finance ongoing operations. Financing a firm's expansion with credit allows the existing owners to avoid bringing in additional investors who would share in the profits. Borrowing can be used to pay for an expansion that will increase the return earned on the owners' investment.

Businesses have an incentive to utilize borrowing because the interest that is paid to lenders can be deducted from income when the businesses calculate their federal and state income taxes. The tax effect of interest expenses causes businesses to favor debt over common stock, on which dividends must be paid with after-tax income. In other words, payments to owners out of a firm's profits cannot be used as a tax deduction.

A substantial amount of long-term business borrowing stipulates a fixed interest rate that permits a business to establish a constant cost of funds for an extended period of time. Businesses often borrow millions of dollars at a fixed rate of interest for twenty-five years or longer. This financial arrangement permits a borrower to determine exactly how many dollars will be required each month or each year to keep a loan current. Businesses frequently have an option to borrow at a variable rate of interest, especially on short-term loans. Loans with variable interest rates do not fix a firm's cost of funds.

The financing mix utilized by businesses of owner contributions and borrowed money varies from industry to industry and from firm to firm. Companies that experience

> Financial advisers counsel against applying for credit at several different sources within a short period of time. Each creditor is likely to access your credit report and cause an inquiry to be recorded in your file. A large number of inquiries may wave a red flag because it indicates you are in the process of a borrowing binge.

relatively stable revenues (predictable sales that do not fluctuate much from quarter to quarter and year to year) are better able to cope with the fixed payments normally required of borrowers. The managers of an electric utility are generally able to forecast the firm's revenues with reasonable accuracy, thereby allowing these firms to utilize substantial amounts of debt to pay for generating plants, transmission facilities, and fuel. On the other hand, businesses like steel manufacturers and mining companies, which have fluctuating revenues that are difficult to forecast accurately, are more at risk when large amounts of debt are used to finance the firm's assets. Companies with fluctuating revenues and substantial amounts of debt will occasionally find it difficult to meet fixed interest and principal payments, especially during a period of weak business activity.

Government borrowing. Governments borrow when tax and fee collections are insufficient to meet spending requirements. Governments at all levels have increasingly relied on borrowed funds to pay for the goods and services their citizens have demanded. Although governments can reduce their reliance on borrowing by reining in spending and/or by increasing taxes, neither option is appealing to lawmakers, who rely on the votes and campaign contributions of taxpayers and recipients of government services and contracts. Citizens lobby to keep open nearby military installa-

> Credit reports are used by employers who evaluate job applicants as well as by creditors who evaluate loan applicants. Thus, it is worthwhile to check on the accuracy of the contents of your credit file even though you don't plan to apply for credit in the near future.

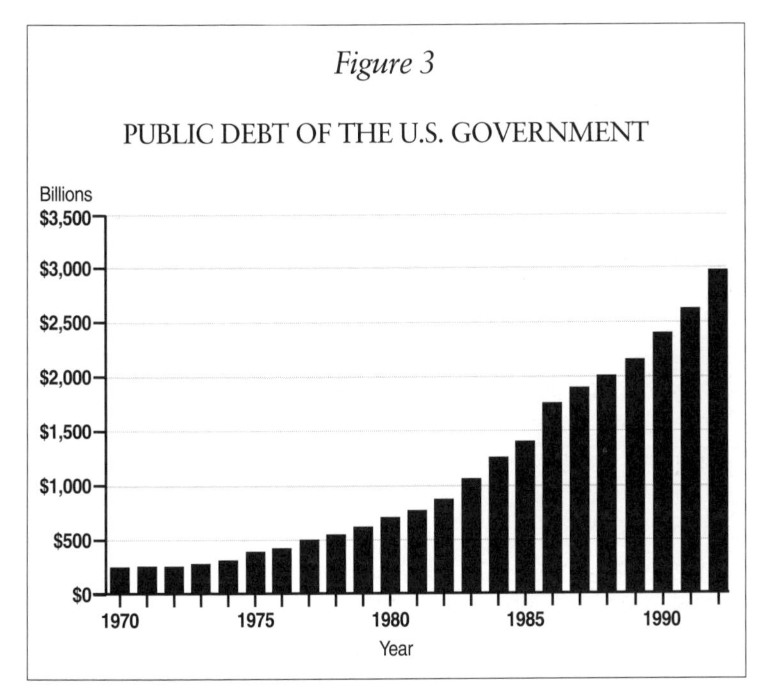

Figure 3

PUBLIC DEBT OF THE U.S. GOVERNMENT

tions and the elderly rail against reductions in Medicare and Social Security payments at the same time that nearly all voters cry "no new taxes." Everyone wants criminals in prison, but only a minority of taxpayers are willing to pay the cost of this incarceration.

A substantial amount of government spending is devoted to the construction or acquisition of bridges, monuments, buildings, equipment, and other long-lasting assets. Anticipated life spans of twenty to thirty years or even longer make it relatively easy to accept that at least a portion of these assets should be financed with borrowed money—an alternative that allows citizens to enjoy the benefits of the assets at the same time that payments are being made on the

If you find yourself needing to use your credit card to pay for things you usually buy for cash, you may be in the credit "danger zone." Consider putting your credit cards in an inconvenient place or doing away with them altogether.

loans. Local citizens derive long-lasting benefits from a new school or recreation complex at the same time that vehicle owners can be expected to enjoy many years of benefits from an improved road system. Of course, governments at all levels have become involved with their share of boondoggles, including unneeded interstate exchanges, airport renovations, and sports stadiums.

Government borrowing to support services and short-term assets that are consumed long before loans are repaid is more worrisome. Borrowing to pay for current social programs, especially programs that can be expected to require even larger financial commitments in future years, presents a long-term problem. Financing short-term government spending requirements with long-term debt commitments (including short-term loans that must be continually renewed) can present long-term financial problems because citizens will be stuck with interest and principal payments long after the government expenditures have occurred and benefits have been exhausted. Long-term borrowing to support short-term spending requirements causes future generations of citizens to pay for the excesses of their parents and grandparents who consumed government resources beyond their willingness to pay the full cost of those resources. Unlike corporate and individual borrowing, a substantial amount of government borrowing takes place with the full intent to "buy now and let someone else pay later."

Personal borrowing. Personal borrowing occurs when an individual is unable to pay for a purchase out of current income and either cannot or does not wish to tap savings. Individuals sometimes borrow directly from a seller but more normally become indebted to a third party, such as a bank or credit union. An individual may use a credit card to purchase gasoline for the car, clothes for the kids, or medicine for family members. A family may take out a credit union loan to purchase an automobile, acquire furniture for the house, or pay for a hospital stay. Individuals also borrow funds that are used to acquire investments or to repay outstanding loans (e.g., borrow from a bank or a credit union to pay off credit card balances or refinance a home loan because interest rates have declined).

While a major proportion of the money borrowed by businesses goes to pay for the purchase of productive assets such as equipment and real estate that will produce revenues to repay the debt, and much government debt is incurred to pay for long-lasting assets (e.g., highways and buildings), personal debt is frequently used to facilitate the purchase of goods and services that are readily consumed. There are exceptions, of course. Houses are long-lasting assets, and vehicles can have extended lives depending on how they are driven and maintained. Still, goods and services purchased by consumers with borrowed money are often long gone while the payments on the loans continue on.

Don't allow credit card balances to remain unpaid when you have savings in the bank. The rate you are paying on a credit card balance is likely to be substantially higher than the rate you are earning on your savings.

CHAPTER 2

Types and Sources of Consumer Credit

Different types of consumer credit are available from a variety of sources. Some loan agreements specify equal monthly or annual payments, while other loans require a single large payment of both principal and interest. Lenders often require that borrowers pledge certain assets as collateral to guarantee repayment of a loan. Some loans require nothing other than a borrower's promise of repayment. Although many lenders provide a full array of loans, some creditors specialize in providing particular types of consumer credit. Individuals interested in borrowing money should shop among several lenders because of wide differences that often exist in credit qualification, fees, and interest rates. A little extra effort may save a substantial sum, especially on large loans with long repayment periods.

Not many years ago a borrower's alternatives were limited, in terms of both the types of lenders that were actively making loans and the variety of loans that were available. Federal and state regulations limited the types of lending that financial institutions could engage in, while at the same time the Federal Reserve restricted the interest rates these institutions could legally pay to depositors. The upper limits on interest rates that could be paid on savings had the effect of artificially reducing the cost of money—both for financial institutions and for customers who borrowed from these institutions—below the level that would have existed in a free market. Financial deregulation during the 1970s and 1980s produced major changes and great turmoil in the financial markets. New players and a dizzying array of innovative credit products offered new alternatives to borrowers.

Types of Consumer Credit

Loans come in greater varieties than crayons. Some loan agreements require that you make a specified number of fixed monthly payments, each comprised of both interest and principal, while other loans require that you pay the lender a single sum on a predetermined date. Some lending agreements specify an interest rate that remains the same throughout the term of a loan, while other loans stipulate a variable interest rate that is periodically altered according to

> Do not become involved with an individual or company that offers to find you a loan in return for your paying an advance fee. Con artists use this ruse to get their hands on your money, after which you are unlikely to see them again.

some identified standard. Some loans require that you pledge certain assets you own as collateral to be claimed by the lender in the event you default on the terms of the loan. Other loans are made on the basis of your promise of repayment.

Installment Credit

Installment credit (also called *closed-end credit)* includes loans that require you to repay the amount borrowed in equal periodic payments, generally monthly. A loan to purchase an automobile or a motor home is an example of installment credit. Installment credit is also a popular method to finance the purchase of refrigerators, washing machines, and other high-end appliances. The lender will ordinarily retain the title (if one exists) to the asset being financed until the loan is completely repaid.

Perhaps you have decided to purchase a $16,000 automobile, using $4,000 from personal savings you have accumulated combined with the proceeds from a $12,000 loan being offered through the dealer. The lender draws up a five-year loan agreement that requires you to make sixty monthly payments of $238. The loan will be paid off (i.e., will have a zero balance) on the date of the last scheduled payment, at which time you will have a clear title to the automobile. The total amount of interest and fees you pay on the loan equals the difference between the sum of all the payments and the amount you borrow. In this example you will pay a total of $14,280 over sixty months (60 months x $238 per month), which includes $2,280 in interest on the principal of $12,000. Each $238 payment you make to the lender is comprised partly of the monthly interest charge and partly of a partial repayment of principal. The composition of interest and principal changes with each scheduled payment as the principal on the loan is reduced. Interest calculations and loan expenses are discussed in more detail in Chapter 4.

Installment credit typically provides little flexibility for a borrower. An installment loan is specifically designed to repay the loan being used to finance a particular asset, and you do not have an option to arbitrarily miss payments or to make payments of a size other than that scheduled in the loan agreement. This doesn't mean you will go to jail or have all your personal assets taken away in the event you miss a car payment. It does mean that you need to contact the lender in the event you will be unable to meet your scheduled payments.

Other Types of Consumer Credit

Noninstallment credit includes single-payment loans and loans that permit you to make irregular payments and to borrow additional funds without submitting a new credit application. The latter category is also called *open-end credit.* Essentially, noninstallment credit applies to all forms of consumer credit other than fixed-payment loans, described in the previous section.

Single-payment loans, also called *term loans,* require that you repay on a specified date the entire amount that was borrowed. A term loan may require periodic interest payments but more likely requires that you pay accumulated interest at the same time you repay the loan's principal. Suppose you borrow $5,000 for one year at 8 percent interest. At the end of the year, you repay the $5,000 that was borrowed plus interest of $400 (8 percent of $5,000 for one year). If the term of the loan was for less than one year, you would owe interest of less than $400, while a loan of more than a year would require interest of more than $400. Single-payment loans are useful if you expect to need the full amount borrowed for a certain length of time.

Open-end credit permits you to borrow as additional funds are needed, so long as you don't accumulate a loan balance that exceeds a predetermined limit. Charge accounts and credit card accounts are the most common examples of open-end credit. Each type of account provides a continuous source of credit. You are permitted to diminish the debt by making payments and to add to the debt by borrowing additional sums, all the while without being required to reapply for credit. Some types of open-end credit require that you repay your entire debt on a particular date, although you can continue to obtain additional funds if your cumulative borrowing hasn't exceeded an amount (your *credit limit,* or *line of credit)* specified in the loan agreement. Other types of open-end credit allow you to make uneven, partial payments subject to a predetermined minimum established by the lender. The minimum payment may be a stipulated dollar amount (e.g., $10 per month) or a percentage of the outstanding balance.

> Streamline your inventory of credit cards. The more credit cards you own, the more likely you are to end up using them and suffering the accompanying credit difficulties, and the more difficult it is to keep track of what you are doing. It is also more likely that you will lose a card, possibly without even missing it!

Charge account. A charge account generally permits a borrower to avoid finance charges by paying the outstanding balance in full within a certain number of days of the billing date. An alternative is to make partial payments and incur interest on the balance. Charge accounts are popular among retailers that hope to stimulate sales at the same time that they earn interest income from customers (e.g., Sears, Roebuck and J. C. Penney). Charge cards are also issued by businesses that desire to build customer loyalty (e.g., oil companies and airlines). Interest rates on charge accounts are generally quite high, making this an expensive source of credit unless you have the discipline and financial resources to repay the entire balance before it begins accruing interest. Charging purchases to your charge account generally makes it easier to return merchandise to a retailer.

Credit card account. Credit card accounts, such as Visa, MasterCard, Discover, and Optima, are the most popular form of open-end credit. Most individuals don't just have a credit card; they have a whole fistful of credit cards. And while credit cards were once sponsored mostly by large banks, cards are now peddled by savings & loan associations, credit unions, automobile manufacturers, and communications firms.

Credit cards can be used to purchase goods and services from merchants or to obtain cash from financial institutions

> If you regularly pay the full balance on your credit card each month, you are receiving an interest-free loan from the card's issuer. Up to two months can elapse between the date you purchase something using your charge card and the date you are required to pay for the purchase.

and automated teller machines. Some card companies charge an annual fee of from $15 to $50 or more, while other cards are issued without an annual charge. Card companies typically permit cardholders to avoid interest charges when an account balance is paid in full by a prescribed date. A variety of methods are utilized to calculate interest charges on credit card accounts, a topic that is discussed in more detail in Chapter 6.

Personal line of credit. A personal line of credit permits you to borrow funds as needed, generally by means of special checks supplied by the lender. The checks can be used to pay for goods and services or to make deposits to your regular checking account. A line of credit permits you to borrow and repay funds at your convenience, subject to a maximum amount that is specified at the time the loan is arranged. Interest charges are based on the amount of the loan and the length of time the funds are borrowed.

Home-equity loan. A home-equity loan uses the equity (i.e., the market value less the balance on any outstanding loans) in your home as collateral and can be structured either as a line of credit or as an installment loan. Home-equity loans are generally restricted to 75 percent of a home's appraised value minus whatever amount is owed to a lender holding a first mortgage. Suppose you purchased a $100,000 home several years ago with a $25,000 down payment and a $75,000 loan. The home has now increased in value to $110,000, and the loan has been paid down to a current balance of $71,000. Using the loan limit just described would allow you to borrow a maximum of $82,500 (75 percent of $110,000), less $71,000, or $11,500.

Home-equity loans are a convenient (some critics would say too convenient) form of borrowing at a competitive short-term interest rate. Once the paperwork is complete, you receive a book of checks to be used in any way you desire. You can write checks for cash or use the checks to pay for merchandise. An additional advantage is that, unlike most other types of consumer loans, interest paid on home-equity loans is allowed as an itemized deduction in calculating your federal income tax liability. Interest on most other types of loans is no longer deductible.

Home-equity loans are easily abused by individuals who lack the discipline to control their spending and borrowing. Just having all that borrowing power available causes some people to spend more money, even if they have to borrow. Another potential disadvantage is that most home-equity loans specify a variable interest rate that can swing upward fairly rapidly, thereby causing the debt to become a greater burden. Pledging your home as collateral for a loan places your primary residence at risk in the event you are unable to meet the required loan payments.

Travel and entertainment (T&E) account. A T&E account, offered by American Express, Diners Club, and other financial services companies, provides credit for a prescribed period, generally thirty days, at which time charges must be paid in full. Credit is accessed by means of charge cards issued by the lender. A T&E account does not permit you to pay only a portion of your bill, as is allowed (actually, encouraged) by credit card companies. Fewer retailers accept T&E cards compared with Visa and MasterCard; at the same time, T&E card issuers are more selective regarding the applicants who are approved to receive their cards.

Thirty-day accounts and service credit. Thirty-day accounts permit customers to defer payment for purchases by up to thirty days without incurring interest charges. Full payment is expected by the due date, and interest is not applicable for this type account. Service credit, offered by utilities, doctors, and other suppliers of services, allows you to make payment fifteen to thirty days following the date a service is provided. For example, you are generally billed by the electric company for electricity you have already consumed. Thus, you are perpetually in debt to the electric company because the payments you make always follow your usage of electricity. Both thirty-day accounts and service credit are offered as a convenience to customers.

Sources of Credit

Specialized lenders were once the standard source of money for home loans, auto loans, and personal loans. You went to a savings & loan for a real estate loan, you visited a commercial bank if you were interested in a loan for your business, you went to a commercial bank or a credit union if you needed a personal loan or an automobile loan, and you headed for a finance company if you were considered a poor credit risk or didn't know any better. Financial deregulation brought new lenders to the credit markets at the same time that it contributed to a blurring of the distinctions among the existing lenders. Savings & loans began making commercial and personal loans, whereas brokerage firms became aggressive real estate lenders. You can now use your home as collateral for a loan to purchase an automobile, borrow from your broker to pay for a vacation, and accumulate credits toward free airline trips when you use your credit card.

Even though lenders are no longer as specialized as in

Figure 4

SOURCES OF CONSUMER CREDIT

Credit Source	Types of Loans	Features
Commercial Banks	Installment loans Single-payment loans Credit card loans Second mortgages	High-quality loans Collateral often required Low interest rates Prefer large loans
Consumer Finance Companies	Installment loans Second mortgages	High interest rates Lower credit standards Small loans Quick decision Many unsecured loans
Credit Unions	Installment loans Credit card loans Second mortgages	Low interest rates Members only Many unsecured loans Small loans
Life Insurance Companies	Loans against cash values	No required payments Low interest rates No fees No credit check required
Savings & Loan Associations	Installment loans Second mortgages Home improvement loans Education loans	High-quality loans Collateral often required
Brokerage Firms	Loans against securities	Must have margin account Variable rates Repay at will Quick access

years past, important differences remain among various financial institutions. Lenders vary in the qualifications they require of borrowers, the interest rates and fees they charge, the types of loans they make available, and the maturity lengths of loans they will make. Being better acquainted with various credit sources will help you determine which lenders are most likely to be sympathetic to your request for a loan.

Commercial Banks

Commercial banks generally offer a greater variety of loans than other lenders. Banks offer installment loans, term loans, and lines of credit, on both a secured and an unsecured basis. Most banks will make loans for the purpose of purchasing a boat, buying a home, taking a vacation, paying off another loan, investing in a business, fixing your roof, or paying your taxes. Commercial banks tend to be choosy lenders, concentrating on making loans to individuals and businesses with an established credit history. This cautious attitude is not universal, and many commercial banks are aggressive lenders. Overly aggressive banks sometimes find themselves with financial difficulties because large number of borrowers default on their obligations to the banks. Banks that concentrate on making high-quality loans suffer fewer losses to defaults and are generally able to offer competitive interest rates.

Savings & Loan Associations

Savings & loan associations (S&Ls) were long restricted to making commercial and residential real estate loans. Nearly all these loans were long-term at fixed interest rates. This was a conservative business that produced steady but modest profits. Financial deregulation has allowed these formerly specialized creditors to diversify their lending practices to the point that many larger S&Ls operate in a manner identical with that of commercial banks. Federal authorities permit savings & loans to make all types of commercial and personal loans. Despite the increased freedom, many savings & loan associations have continued to concentrate on making real estate loans.

Credit Unions

Credit unions are cooperative associations that accept savings from and make loans to individuals who have some affiliation, generally a common place of employment. Individuals who qualify for membership in a credit union must purchase a credit union share (e.g., make a small deposit of $5.00 or so) to activate their membership status and participate in the financial services that are offered. If your employer does not sponsor a credit union, you may qualify for membership in another nearby credit union.

Credit unions tend to concentrate on making installment loans, especially for automobile purchases. Home-equity loans and unsecured personal loans are also offered by most

> Don't overlook your life insurance policy as a source of low-cost credit. You can often borrow money more cheaply from your life insurance policy than from a financial institution. Also, life insurance loans have the advantage of not imposing a deadline when you must repay the loan.

credit unions. Larger credit unions make mortgage loans on residential real estate, although the maximum loan amount may be smaller than could be obtained at a savings & loan association. Low overhead costs that are frequently partially subsidized by their sponsors often permit credit unions to offer loans at relatively low rates compared with what you would pay at a commercial bank or savings & loan association. Collection costs, slow repayments, and defaults are reduced at credit unions, since they typically withhold loan payments from a borrower's paycheck. Volunteer work by members serves to further reduce the expenses incurred by credit unions.

Consumer Finance Companies

Consumer finance companies concentrate on making installment loans and second mortgages. Loans that allow borrowers to repay outstanding loans are also popular among customers of consumer finance companies. Consumer finance companies are more willing to make relatively small loans that commercial banks and savings & loan associations generally avoid. These lenders charge relatively high interest rates and are more likely than other lenders to approve loans for applicants with woeful credit histories or no prior borrowing experience. The worse an individual's credit history, the greater the amount of security that may be required by a lender before approving a loan. Borrowers can pledge additional collateral in an attempt to negotiate for reduced interest rates on loans.

High interest rates and excessive fees make consumer finance companies a relatively undesirable credit source. If you have unencumbered assets (i.e., assets that are not being used for collateral on another loan) and/or a history of responsible credit use, you can almost surely obtain a better deal on a loan at a commercial bank or an S&L than at a consumer finance company. Even if you don't consider yourself a particularly good credit risk, you should at least make an effort to talk to a bank when you are interested in borrowing money.

Sales Finance Companies

Sales finance companies are formed to lend money to customers of an affiliated company. For example, General Motors Acceptance Corporation (GMAC) acts as a credit source to car buyers at General Motors dealerships. GMAC borrows money in the financial markets and, in turn, lends it to consumers. Sales finance companies periodically offer borrowers particularly attractive interest rates to stimulate business at the affiliated company. For example, Volkswagen of America's affiliated finance company once offered financing at 3.9 percent annual interest to buyers of new Volkswagen vehicles. Without special financing, loans at sales finance companies are likely to be convenient, but more expensive than similar loans at commercial banks and credit unions.

Life Insurance Companies

Life insurance companies are a source of credit for certain policyholders who own life insurance policies that include a savings component, or *cash value.* Savings accumulate in a life insurance policy when scheduled payments, or *premiums,* exceed the cost of the death benefits that are being purchased by the policyholder. In general, life insurance policies with constant premiums include a savings feature, even though the premiums typically must be paid for many years before a cash value of significant size is available for borrowing. Term insurance, an inexpensive form of life insurance that provides a death benefit but no savings or cash values, cannot be used for loans by policyholders.

Life insurance loans often carry relatively low interest rates compared with the rates you would be charged on other types of consumer loans. The determination of the rate you will be required to pay to borrow funds from your life insurance will be specified in the policy. You should realize that life insurance loans involve borrowing your own money (i.e., you borrow savings that have accumulated in the policy) and that any loan outstanding at the time of your death will be deducted from the policy's death benefit. Still, borrowing from a life insurance policy that has accumulated a cash value is an alternative that should be considered when you are shopping for a loan.

Brokerage Firms

Brokerage firms are a source of credit when you have securities on deposit in a margin account. The maximum you are permitted to borrow depends on the market value of the securities you own and the percentage of this value the brokerage firm will lend. You are generally permitted to borrow

> A cash advance on your credit card is a convenient way to obtain money, but it is often expensive. Try to save this option for emergencies when there are no other sources of cash.

approximately 70 percent of the current market value of your securities. Although there is no specific date on which you must repay the loan, you may be required to put up additional collateral if there is a decline in the market value of the securities in your account. Money that you borrow against securities you own may be used for any purpose, not just for investment needs.

Pawnbrokers

Pawnbrokers offer short-term, single-payment loans secured with personal property that you leave with the lender. The pawnbroker has the right to sell your property in the event you are unable to repay the loan and accumulated interest on the scheduled date. Pawnbrokers provide quick access to cash for individuals who have poor credit and no alternative source of funds. On the downside, pawnbroker loans tend to be very expensive because they have very high rates of interest.

Friends and Relatives

If you have been turned down for a loan by several banks and you consider the interest rate being charged by the local finance companies you have visited to be too high, you may decide that your only real alternative is to seek financial assistance from a relative or close friend. Perhaps you will be able to borrow at a favorable interest rate and still provide your relative or friend with a superior investment return. Sounds good, but . . .

Borrowing from a relative or friend may allow you to obtain favorable repayment terms, but at the expense of damaging your personal relationship, especially if you are unable to meet the terms of the loan or if you and the other individual have a misunderstanding concerning the terms of the loan. Personal loans from relatives or friends frequently have unclear terms that can be subject to different interpretations. You should also be aware that moving to a debtor-creditor association can change a relationship in which two people have been equals. Borrowing from a friend or relative may allow you to obtain a low interest rate but potentially at a high cost of another kind.

CHAPTER 3

The Cost of Borrowing

Interest and fees charged on a loan have the effect of increasing the cost of a good or service purchased with credit. Various methods that are used to calculate interest rates can mislead a borrower about the cost of a loan. The interest rate charged on a loan depends on numerous factors, including the length of the loan, the value and liquidity of security pledged as collateral, the borrower's credit history, and the price the lender must pay for the money that is being loaned. Interest rates are also influenced by economic activity and government policy. Wide variations in interest rates charged by lenders make it worthwhile for a borrower to shop carefully for a loan.

Individuals sometimes spend weeks or months shopping for the best deal on an automobile or some other good and then squander their hard-earned savings by accepting whatever terms are offered to finance the purchase. Financing costs often comprise a substantial portion of the overall cost of a purchase so that it is important to understand how the financing costs are calculated and actions you can take to reduce these costs.

Some Facts about Interest Rates

The interest rate you must pay to borrow money is influenced by many factors relating to the particular type of loan you choose. The length of time a loan is to be outstanding, the collateral, your credit history, and the lender you choose are all important determinants of the interest rate you will be charged on a loan. Interest rates are also influenced by factors outside your control and unrelated to the specifics of your particular loan. No matter how much collateral you offer and how painstakingly you search among lenders for the most favorable terms on a loan, you will almost surely be unable to finance your home at an interest rate of under 4 percent. Likewise, you will be unable to obtain a 3 percent car loan or a 2 percent loan from your broker no matter how good your credit. The importance of outside influences on interest rates doesn't mean that the details of your partic-

Lenders are required by law to tell you the cost of credit (interest and other charges) and the terms of repayment before you borrow money.

ular loan don't count for much in determining the interest rate you pay. It does mean that conditions in the credit market play a major role in the terms of any loan you obtain.

The Importance of Economic Activity

Economic conditions have an important influence on interest rates. Interest rates tend to increase during periods of strong economic activity when credit demand is high. A vigorous economy causes businesses to borrow funds that can be used to expand their output. At the same time, high employment and wage increases that accompany economic expansion are likely to put consumers in an optimistic mood, leading them to buy more goods and services on credit. Credit demand that accompanies a strong economy allows lenders to increase the interest rates they charge on loans; it also causes these lenders to have to pay higher returns to attract savers' money.

An economy mired in weakness does little to stimulate demand for credit by businesses or consumers. Periods of weak economic activity are accompanied by idle manufacturing capacity, causing a decline in credit needs by most businesses, which are in no mood to expand. Likewise, a weak economy and rising unemployment cause consumers to become cautious and cut back on their spending and borrowing. The slack demand for credit during periods of weak economic activity tends to cause a decline in interest rates.

The Importance of Inflationary Expectations

Consumer, business, and government inflationary expectations have an important influence on the level of interest

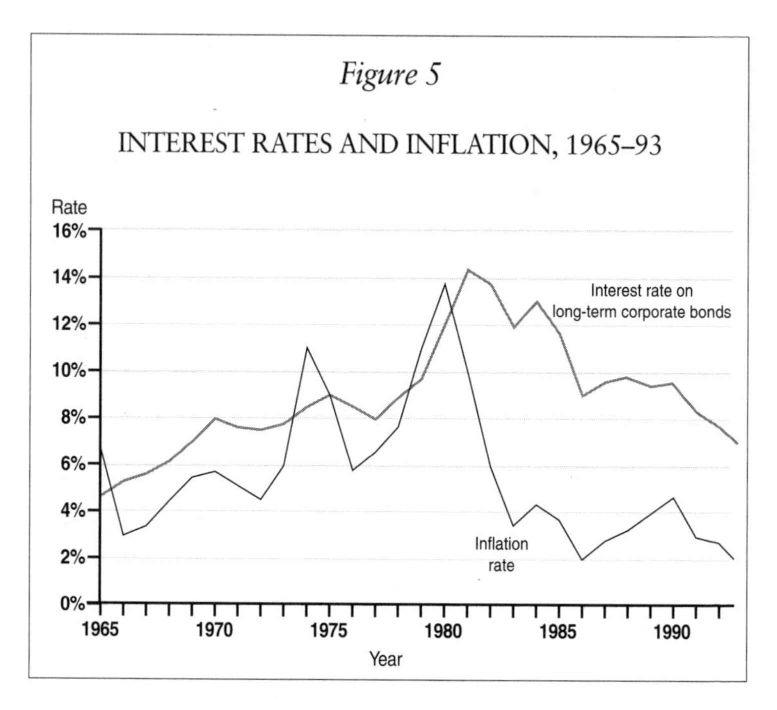

rates. Lenders that anticipate rising prices for goods and services will attempt to charge higher interest rates in order to seek compensation for the likelihood that loans will be repaid with devalued dollars. A lender that anticipates an 8 percent inflation rate is not inclined to willingly suffer a loss of purchasing power by making loans at an interest rate of 6 percent.

At the same time that lenders view inflation as a reason to charge higher interest rates, potential borrowers, anticipating a high inflation rate, are likely to accept loans with higher interest rates because they expect to be able to repay lenders with devalued dollars. Inflation is often accompanied by rising consumer income and business revenues that make it easier for borrowers to repay their debt obligations. Anticipation of rising inflation also stimulates consumers and businesses to buy as soon as possible in order to beat expected price increases. Accelerated purchases by consumers and businesses increase the demand for credit, which, in turn, drives interest rates upward.

The Importance of Government Policy

Policies and actions of the federal government have a major impact on interest rates. Large federal deficits that result when federal expenditures exceed tax revenues require the government to annually borrow tens or hundreds of billions of dollars. Large amounts of government borrowing can cause great strains on the credit markets by grabbing loanable funds away from businesses and consumers. During the late 1980s and early 1990s, annual federal deficits of *hundreds of billions* of dollars caused the government to have to borrow huge amounts of money that could otherwise have been available to businesses and individuals. Large government deficits increase the demand for credit and exert upward pressure on interest rates.

The federal government continually intervenes in the credit markets to influence interest rates and guide the nation's economic activity. Government intervention is orchestrated by the Federal Reserve Board (Fed), an independent agency headed by presidential appointees. The Federal Re-

> Except in unusual circumstances, you should avoid the purchase of credit insurance when you borrow. Credit life insurance is generally very expensive for the coverage you receive.

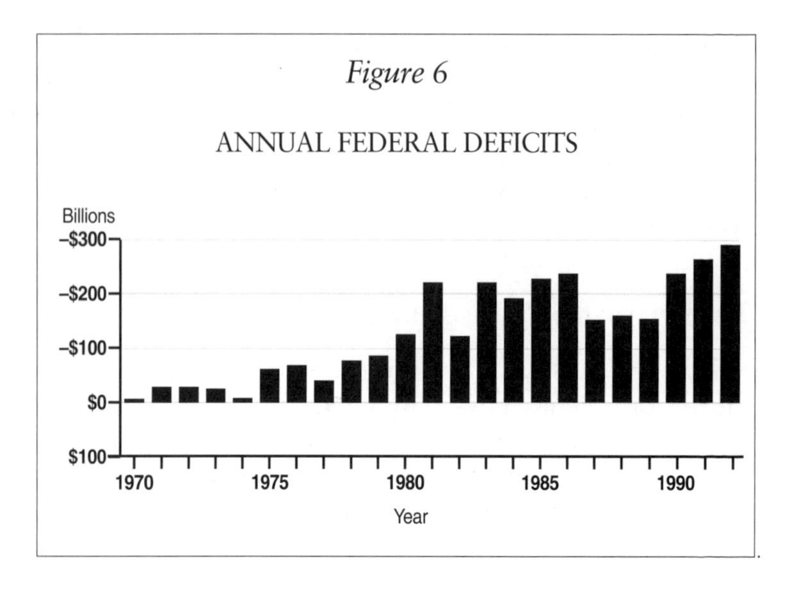

Figure 6

ANNUAL FEDERAL DEFICITS

serve acts as a banker to commercial banks. It clears checks, makes loans, and sets the amount of reserves that member banks must maintain. The Federal Reserve has several tools at its disposal for affecting the credit markets.

- The Federal Reserve sets the interest rate (called the *discount rate)* that commercial banks must pay when they borrow from the Fed. Commercial banks borrow when they need reserves or additional funds for making loans. A change in the discount rate is likely to cause commercial banks to change the interest rates they charge on loans to business and individual borrowers.
- The Fed is constantly buying and selling Treasury securities in the financial markets. These transactions (called *open-market operations)* have a major impact on the money supply, credit availability, and interest rates. A large purchase of Treasury securities by the Federal Re-

serve causes new funds to flow into the banking system, which then has more funds to lend. The additional funds generally cause a decline in interest rates. A large sale of Treasury securities absorbs deposits and reserves from the banking system, thereby causing banks to increase interest rates and cut back on lending.

- Public announcements by members of the Federal Reserve can have powerful effects on the credit markets. If a board member indicates that the Fed is concerned about a resumption of inflation, interest rates are likely to rise in anticipation of efforts by the Federal Reserve to tighten credit.

The Importance of Maturity Length

A loan's maturity length (i.e., the length of time before the loan is totally repaid) generally affects the rate of interest that will be charged. Loans with longer maturities typically have higher interest rates. You will generally be required to pay a higher interest rate on a thirty-year home mortgage than you will on a fifteen-year home mortgage on the same house for the same amount. You are also likely to have to pay a higher interest rate on a five-year car loan than on a three-year car loan. The direct relationship between the maturity length and interest rates for U.S. Treasury securities that is illustrated in Figure 7 is applicable to most types of government, individual, and business borrowing.

> If you live in a community property state, a creditor may consider your spouse's credit history even if you are applying for credit in your own name.

Figure 7

MATURITIES AND INTEREST RATES

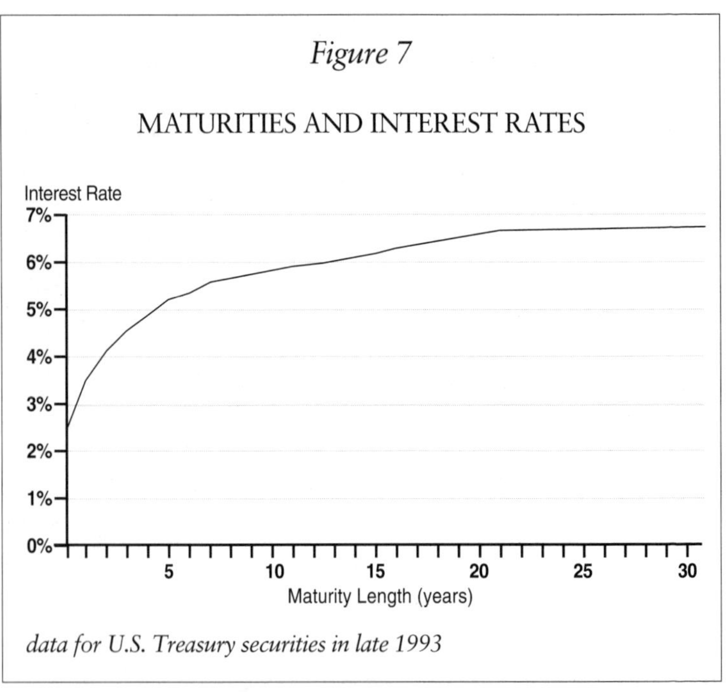

data for U.S. Treasury securities in late 1993

A loan with a long repayment period places the lender at greater risk. A lender finds it much more difficult to evaluate a borrower's ability and willingness to repay a thirty-year loan than a loan scheduled for repayment in six months. Even company officers who have an intimate knowledge of their firm's operations will have less than total confidence in a thirty-year forecast. The task is much tougher for lenders that have less familiarity with the firm.

Unanticipated inflation can cause major losses in purchasing power for lenders that make long-term loans. Imagine making a loan at a 6 percent interest rate for twenty years and finding several years later that annual inflation had increased to 9 percent. The funds that are due from the borrower will be deteriorating so rapidly in value that you will lose purchasing power during each year the loan is outstanding. Anticipated inflation is built into the terms of a loan (i.e., it is included in the interest rate), but unanticipated inflation can prove devastating to a lender, especially over a long period of time.

The positive relationship between Treasury maturities and interest rates displayed in Figure 7 does not always carry over to consumer and business loans. For example, loans with similar terms but different collateral are likely to have different interest rates. A one-year personal loan without collateral may have a higher interest rate than a three-year car loan, because the car provides the lender with added security. Likewise, a six-month personal loan may carry a higher interest rate than a one-year personal loan, so as to allow the lender to recover expenses that are incurred in making the loan (e.g., employee time, paperwork, and credit research).

The Importance of Collateral

The potential for a borrower to default on a loan is one of the chief risks faced by a lender. Companies periodically encounter poor business conditions, and individuals occasionally lose their jobs. Both possibilities make it less likely that outstanding debts will be fully repaid. A lender holding only a borrower's promise stands to lose a substantial amount of money in the event the borrower is unable to meet the terms of the loan. Although a lender has legal avenues to attempt to recover the principal of the loan, the borrower may have several other loans and few assets of any value.

A borrower who pledges specific assets as collateral for a loan places the lender in a more secure financial position. In the event the borrower is unable to repay the loan, the lender can force the sale of the collateral and utilize the funds to make up the unpaid interest and remaining balance on the loan. Collateral that improves a lender's financial position should result in a reduced interest rate. The greater the value of the collateral compared with the amount borrowed, the less the risk to the lender and the more the interest rate on the loan should be reduced.

The Cost of Borrowing

Suppose you are offered a six-month $5,000 loan to be repaid in six monthly installments of $900 each. Total repayments amount to $5,400 (6 x $900), meaning that you will be charged interest of $5,400 (the total amount of the payments) less $5,000 (the amount you borrow), or $400. The lender tells you the loan offers an attractive interest rate of $400/$5,000 (the amount of interest to be paid divided by the amount borrowed), or 8 percent. In fact, is 8 percent an accurate interest rate quotation for this loan, or are you being hoodwinked by the lender?

Calculating Interest Rates

In the simplest case, the interest rate on a loan is calculated as the dollar amount of interest you are charged divided by the amount of money borrowed. If you borrow $1,000 that must be repaid at the end of one year along with $60 in interest, you are being charged an interest rate of $60/$1,000, or 6 percent. The general formula for calculating the interest rate on a loan is:

$$i = I/P$$

where

i is the interest rate
I is the dollar amount of interest paid
P is the amount borrowed

In real life most loans are more complicated than this example. Loans often involve a term of other than one year, and many loans are repaid with a series of payments rather than with a single payment. Some loans require periodic interest payments by the borrower until a predetermined date, when the entire amount borrowed becomes due. Because the specifics of loans can differ so much, it is worthwhile to familiarize yourself with some of the more important conventions and details that affect the interest rate.

Interest rates are quoted on an annual basis. Certain financial variables, including inflation, investment returns, and interest rates, are nearly always computed and quoted on an annual, or yearly, basis. An adjustment is required to annualize the interest rate for loans of other than one year. Suppose you borrow $1,000 and sign a loan agreement that requires you to repay $1,060 in *three months*. You are paying the same dollar interest required by the one-year loan agreement discussed above, but now you have use of the borrowed money for only three months rather than a full

> Using your home as collateral for a succession of loans can be unwise, since you may end up at retirement with so much debt that you cannot afford to quit work. You should make plans to have your home loan paid off several years before you plan to retire.

year. The interest rate on this loan must be annualized to account for the short term. First, divide the number of months the loan is scheduled to be outstanding (in this case, three months) into the number of months in a year (always twelve). The result (12/3 = 4) is multiplied by the interest rate calculated from the previous formula. The annualized rate for the three-month loan is ($60/$1,000) x (12 months/3 months), or 6 percent times four, or 24 percent; the same amount borrowed, the same dollar amount of interest paid, for one-fourth the time, means four times the interest rate. If $60 in interest is charged for a $1,000 loan that is to be repaid in two years, the annualized interest rate would be ($60/$1,000) x (12 months/24 months), or 3 percent. You must always make certain that you and a lender are using the same assumptions in discussing the interest rate on a loan.

A loan's repayment schedule may have a significant impact on the interest rate you pay. Suppose you borrow $2,400 for one year. At the end of the year, you are to repay the amount borrowed plus $240 interest. This arrangement permits you to retain control of the entire amount borrowed ($2,400) for a full year. A requirement to pay interest or a portion of the principal prior to the loan's maturity causes an increase in a loan's effective rate of interest. Suppose an alternative loan agreement to borrow the same $2,400 requires twelve monthly payments of $220 each. You still repay a total of $2,640, the same as with the single-payment obligation, but this alternative requires a payment of interest and a gradual repayment of the *principal* during the term of the loan. The monthly principal repayments cause you to control a decreasing amount of borrowed money over the course of the loan. A loan agreement in which the total

Figure 8

EFFECTIVE INTEREST RATE FOR DIFFERENT LOAN PAYMENT SCHEDULES

Suppose you approach several different lenders with the same request: to borrow $3,000 for one year. Each lender quotes an interest rate of 10 percent but offers different repayment plans.

Lender 1 The lender adds interest of $300 to the loan principal of $3,000 and requires you to make a single payment of $3,300 at the end of one year.

Lender 2 The lender gives you $3,000 and requires 12 equal monthly payments of $265.85. Each payment takes care of the monthly interest charge and causes a slight reduction in the amount owed.

Lender 3 Lender adds $300 interest to $3,000 borrowed and divides by 12 to obtain monthly payments of $3,300/12, or $275. You receive $3,000.

Lender 4 Lender keeps interest of $300 and gives you $2,700. Payments are set at $3,000/12, or $250.

Lender	Amount Borrowed	Payments	Total Payments	Total Interest Paid	Approximate Interest Rate
1	$3,000	$3,300	$3,300	$300	10.00%
2	3,000	263.75/month	3,165	190	10.15
3	3,000	275.00/month	3,300	300	18.46
4	2,700	250.00/month	3,000	300	20.51

amount of interest is added to the amount borrowed, and the sum is divided by the number of payments to determine the size of each payment, is known as the *add-on interest method.*

Given the choice of paying $2,640 at the end of the year or $220 per month for one year, which should you choose? Or does it really matter? It is to your advantage to choose the single payment of $2,640 because you pay the same dollar amount of interest ($240) but have, on average, a larger amount of money borrowed. Add-on interest increases the effective cost of a loan.

Interest collected on a loan's front-end increases the effective interest rate. Certain installment loans, known as *discount loans,* are structured to allow the lender to collect the total amount of the interest at the time the loan is made. The effect of a discount loan is to charge interest on money that will not be available to the borrower. Suppose you borrow $1,500 for two years at a quoted rate of 8 percent. The lender deducts $240 in interest charges (8 percent x $1,500 x 2 years) and writes you a check for $1,260, the balance of $1,500. The loan obligates you to pay twenty-four monthly installments of $62.50 each. Quoting 8 percent interest for this loan is misleading. First, monthly payments require you to repay interest charges and a portion of the principal each

Arrange for financing ahead of the time you actually need the money. Having a lender's commitment allows you to shop for the best deal on whatever it is you are intending to purchase. Being in a hurry to obtain a loan because you need the money right away is likely to cause you to accept whatever loan terms are offered by a lender.

month. Repaying principal throughout the term of the loan means you do not have the use of all that you have borrowed for the full term. Second, interest is being charged on $1,500 even though you actually receive only $1,260 from the lender. Discounted interest increases the effective interest rate by requiring you to pay interest on more money than you receive.

Interest can be calculated on a simple or a compounded basis. Suppose you are interested in obtaining a $4,000 three-year loan. One bank offers the loan at a 12 percent annual interest rate with principal and total interest of $1,440 (12 percent x $4,000 x 3 years) to be paid at the end of three years. Interest calculated only on the original principal of a loan is known as *simple interest.* A second bank offers a loan at the same stated rate but requires that you pay $40 interest at the end of each of thirty-six months. The last interest payment is to be accompanied by repayment of the $4,000 principal. Paying interest monthly, or, alternatively, having the lender calculate interest in each subsequent month on both principal and accumulated interest is known as *compounding*. Compounding increases the effective rate of interest earned by savers (e.g., a savings account pays you interest quarterly or semiannually rather than annually) and increases the cost of borrowed money.

Creditors sometimes use different loan balances to calculate interest charges. It has already been pointed out that creditors sometimes calculate interest on the amount borrowed even though installment payments will gradually reduce the balance that is owed over the life of the loan. Credit card companies also utilize several methods to calculate the interest charged to cardholders. Some issuers credit any payments you have made before calculating your finance charges. It is to your advantage to receive credit for payments you have made because the credit reduces the loan balance on which interest is calculated. Other credit card issuers calculate interest for a given period without considering payments you have made during the period. This method works to your disadvantage because a higher loan balance is used to calculate your interest charges. Still other credit card issuers charge interest that is based on the average daily balance of your borrowing. All these different methods of calculating interest on credit card balances is discussed more fully in Chapter 6. Suffice it to say that the interest you are assessed on a credit card balance depends to a large degree on the calculation method used by the issuer. The method of calculating interest is of little consequence if you regularly pay off your credit card balance in full each month.

Purchasing credit insurance increases the cost of a loan. Many lenders attempt to convince borrowers to purchase credit insurance that ensures repayment of a loan in the event the borrower dies, becomes disabled, or suffers a loss of property. The premium cost of the insurance is added to the amount being financed so that a borrower ends up paying interest on this additional expense. Credit insurance is a

> Borrow only as much money as you require. Just because a creditor will lend you 85 percent of the purchase price of a new automobile doesn't mean you should necessarily borrow this much. Extra funds you have available to increase the down payment on a loan (i.e., decrease the amount borrowed) can result in substantial interest savings. Borrowing a reduced amount improves the lender's position and will sometimes allow you to obtain a loan at a slightly lower interest rate.

profitable financial product that is aggressively sold by many lenders, and such insurance is sometimes required to gain approval for a loan. Credit insurance also benefits lenders, in that they don't have to be concerned about how a loan will be repaid in the event the borrower dies or becomes disabled. Many financial advisers suggest that credit insurance is a luxury most borrowers should decline.

The Annual Percentage Rate: A Comparable Measure of Interest

Because several different calculations can be used to come up with an interest rate quotation, it is fortunate that there is an accepted standard for computing the cost of borrowing money. A standardized calculation allows you to compare the interest rates being offered by different lenders. Without a standardized method of calculation, it is difficult to know for certain whether the lowest quoted rate is, in fact, the lowest actual rate.

The standard measure of the cost of borrowing is known as the *annual percentage rate (APR)*. Knowing the annual percentage rate is useful regardless of whether you are in the market for an installment loan or a single-payment loan. The *Consumer Credit Protection Act of 1968* (also called the *Truth in Lending Law*) requires that all creditors, including banks, savings & loan associations, car dealers, retailers, finance companies, and credit card companies, provide a borrower with a loan's total finance charges and annual percentage rate. These two pieces of information give you the ammunition you need to compare the offerings of various lenders. Remember, interest rates are comparable only when they have been calculated in the same manner.

Figure 9

CALCULATING THE ANNUAL PERCENTAGE RATE FOR A LOAN

A loan's annual percentage rate can be closely approximated using the following formula.

$$i = \frac{2 \times n \times I}{P(N + 1)}$$

where

- i is the annual percentage rate
- n is the number of payment periods in one year
- I is the total financing charges (mostly interest)
- P is the principal (the amount borrowed)
- N is the number of scheduled payments

Suppose you borrow $12,000 to purchase a used Nissan 300ZX and the loan is to be repaid in 48 monthly payments of $300 each. Each payment covers monthly interest plus a portion of the outstanding balance on the loan. The total payments required by the loan agreement amount to 48 x $300, or $14,400. The loan's total dollar cost of credit equals the total of your payments ($14,400) less the amount you borrow ($12,000), or $2,400. The APR on the loan is calculated as follows:

$$\frac{2 \times 12 \times \$2{,}400}{\$12{,}000(48 + 1)} = 9.8 \text{ percent}$$

Now it is time to review the question posed earlier in this chapter. To refresh your memory, you are being offered a $5,000 loan that requires six monthly payments of $900 each. The lender tells you that you will be paying 8 percent interest, as calculated by dividing the total interest charge ($5,400 less $5,000, or $400) by the amount borrowed ($5,000). One problem is that the lender is requiring that you repay the loan in installments but quoting an interest rate based on your having the full amount of the loan available for the entire six months. Also, the lender has failed to annualize the rate to adjust for the scheduled payoff in six months, not one year.

Using the APR formula presented in Figure 9, the interest rate on this loan is calculated as

$$i = \frac{2 \times 12 \times \$400}{\$5{,}000(6 + 1)} = \frac{\$9{,}600}{\$35{,}000} = 27.4 \text{ percent}$$

This calculation presents quite a different picture of the relative cost of the loan compared with the 8 percent rate that has been quoted by the lender.

Early Repayment of a Loan

Perhaps you have received a fat raise or inherited money from your deceased aunt's estate and decide to repay a loan before its scheduled due date. The early repayment should reduce your total financing costs because the bank will have its money returned ahead of schedule. On the other hand, will you be required to compensate the lender, who stands to lose interest income because of your early repayment?

Potential penalties and rebates in financing costs caused by a loan's early repayment should be addressed in the contract you sign when the loan is made. Some agreements permit you to prepay a loan without penalty. Suppose you borrow $5,000 for one year, with interest and principal to be repaid in one single end-of-year payment. If you decide to repay the loan at the end of six months, you will be charged only half the scheduled finance charges.

The Rule of 78s

The amount required for early repayment of an installment loan is more difficult to compute than that for a single-payment loan, because installment loans involve series of equal payments that are allocated partly to interest and partly to principal reduction. When an installment loan is to be repaid early, the lender must determine how much of the remaining payments represent financing charges to be deducted in calculating the payoff. If you intend to pay off a loan that has fifteen remaining payments of $400 each, you should not be required to repay fifteen times $400, or $6,000, because a significant portion of these payments represent interest that should not be charged.

Lenders frequently use the *rule of 78s* to determine the amount that must be paid by a borrower who wishes to repay an installment loan ahead of schedule. The rule of 78s provides a method to calculate the amount of interest that is

> If credit availability causes you to purchase things you would ordinarily not buy, you may be better off canceling some of your credit arrangements, including your credit cards.

Figure 10

CALCULATING AN EARLY LOAN PAYOFF USING THE RULE OF 78s

Suppose you borrow $9,000 and sign a loan agreement that calls for 24 monthly payments of $500 each. The financing charges over the life of the loan equal the total of your scheduled payments ($12,000) less the amount you borrow ($10,000), or $2,000. After a year and a half (18 months) you decide that the extra cash in a savings account is paying such a paltry return that you may as well withdraw the savings and pay off the balance of the loan.

According to the rule of 78s, the lender will calculate your required payment by determining the sum of the digits for all the scheduled payments (e.g., 24 + 23 + 22 + . . . + 1, or 300) and the sum of the digits for the remaining payments (e.g., 6 + 5 + 4 + 3 + 2 + 1, or 21). The fraction determined by dividing the sum of the digits for the remaining payments (21) by the sum of the digits of the entire loan (300) is multiplied by the total finance charge ($2,000) to determine the scheduled interest you *should not have to pay* because the loan will be paid off early. This reduction in interest is subtracted from the sum of all the remaining payments to determine the amount you will be required to pay in order to retire the debt after 18 months.

The fraction of total interest that should be forgiven because of early repayment is as follows:

$$\frac{\text{sum of the digits of remaining payments}}{\text{sum of the digits of all payments}} = \frac{21}{300} = .070$$

Scheduled interest included in the last 6 payments that should be forgiven is equal to the fraction calculated above times the total financing charge, or

$$.070 \times \$2{,}000 = \$140.00$$

The amount to pay off the loan early is equal to the sum of the remaining payments less the amount of interest that is included in the payments, or

$$(6 \times \$500) - \$140 = \$2{,}860$$

embodied in all the remaining installment payments. For example, if you are scheduled to make an additional twelve monthly payments of $400 each and the rule of 78s determines that interest of $500 is included in these payments, you will be required to come up with twelve times $400, or $4,800, less $500, or $4,300. Figure 10 illustrates the calculation used to determine the early payoff on a loan using the rule of 78s.

CHAPTER 4

Obtaining a Loan

Planning and persistence are sometimes required to locate a lender who is willing to provide you with a loan. Proper preparation on your part increases the likelihood that you will locate a lender and obtain a loan on the most favorable terms. You should determine the type of loan you need and identify the lenders that are most likely to make this type of loan. You should also assemble certain personal information that the lender will need in order to make a decision on your loan request. The better able you are to convince a lender that you will repay the loan, the more likely you are to receive a favorable decision on your loan application.

Knowing how and where to search for a lender and how best to apply for a loan increases the likelihood that you will be successful in obtaining the money you seek. Chapter 2 identified various categories of lenders and their respective lending specialties. This information will help you to concentrate your search among creditors that are most likely to be offering the type of loan you are seeking. Don't waste both your time and lenders' time by wandering from one financial institution to another without regard to the kinds of loans these firms make.

Once you have identified several likely sources of money, determine the most effective way to approach each of these prospects. Begin by imagining yourself on the opposite side of the lending desk. If you were the lender, what considerations would be important in deciding whether to make the loan? What kinds of information would you request? You would surely want to know if the applicant has other loans outstanding, including the payments and the amounts owed. The amount, sources, and stability of the applicant's income would help you assess the applicant's ability to service current debts plus the added burden of an additional loan. A modest income combined with relatively heavy debt payments typically signals trouble and casts doubt on the applicant's ability to handle even more debt. You are likely to want a record of the applicant's job history, on the theory

Always apply for credit using exactly the same name. For example, if you normally include your middle initial, always include your middle initial. Using the same name will result in a more accurate reporting of your credit history in credit bureau files.

that employment stability increases the likelihood that the terms of a loan agreement will be honored. The types of information you would request from a loan applicant are probably very similar to information a lender will request from you.

Identifying the Loan You Prefer

Shopping for a loan is in many ways similar to shopping for a washing machine, an automobile, a new home, or a frozen pizza. You set out to locate a particular good or service that best satisfies your needs at the lowest possible cost. Loans, like most goods and services, are offered in several forms, from the most basic to the very fancy, and at widely varying prices. Just as you must determine which make and model of washing machine best satisfies your laundry needs (size, color, electronic vs. manual controls, etc.), so too should you identify the type of loan that best meets your particular borrowing requirements. Some of the basic decisions you should come to grips with before seeking a lender include the following:

How much you wish to borrow. The first thing you need to determine is the amount of money you need. This requires you to estimate the cost of whatever it is you intend to buy or do. What is the cost of the new car, the summer-long vacation, private school tuition, your dream home, or the payoff on your credit card. Can you imagine sitting across from a lender who asks, "How much money do you want to borrow?" and, with a puzzled look, replying, "Gee, I'm not quite sure." Impressive, huh?

The length of time you need the money. Do you need the

money for a month, six months, a year, or twenty years? Perhaps you need $2,500 to pay college tuition and expect to be able to repay a loan within a month, when financial aid will be approved. If the aid isn't forthcoming you feel that you should be able to pay off the loan and finance charges by the end of one year. On the other hand, perhaps you are planning to purchase a new home and require a loan of twenty years or more. Your ability to make the required payments will be a major factor in determining an appropriate maturity. The more income you will have available to meet loan payments, the shorter the maturity you can handle.

Your preferred method of repayment. Would you prefer to retire the loan with a series of equal monthly payments, or would you rather repay the entire amount of the loan in one lump sum? If you chose the single-payment option, would you prefer to pay interest charges annually, or would you rather have interest charges accumulate until the date the loan is scheduled to be repaid? You should build some flexibility into your repayment preference because you may find that your preference is unrealistic in the eyes of the lenders. For example, you can expect to encounter difficulty locating a lender that makes a single-payment car loan.

The Things Lenders Consider Important

As previously mentioned, lenders are primarily interested in whether a potential borrower is likely to fulfill the requirements of a loan agreement. A lender will be more disposed to act favorably on your loan application if you are viewed as someone who will make a full and timely repayment. Re-

Figure 11

WHAT CREDITORS CANNOT DO

When you apply for credit, a creditor cannot:

- ask whether you are divorced or widowed
- ask about your plans for having or raising children
- discourage you from applying because of your sex, marital status, age, or national origin, or because you receive public assistance income
- ask about your marital status if you are applying for a separate, unsecured account and you *do not* live in a community property state
- ask for information about your spouse unless the spouse will have access to the account or you will be relying on your spouse's income to support your application
- consider your age, except when you are underage or when the creditor favors you because of your age

When deciding to give you credit, a creditor cannot:

- consider your sex, marital status, race, national origin, or religion
- consider the race of the people who live in the neighborhood where you want to buy or improve a house with borrowed money
- refuse to consider income from public assistance, part-time employment, pensions, or consistently received alimony or child support payments

member, a creditor lends you money in the expectation of earning a profit—an unlikely outcome if there is a good possibility that you will default on a loan.

Lenders vary in their ways of evaluating loan applicants.

Indeed, an individual lender may use different methods to evaluate different applicants. Some lenders may emphasize personal qualities as evidenced from a personal interview and contacts with references. Other lenders strictly follow a list of established guidelines related to income, length of employment, current debts and loan payments, family size, and so forth. Many lenders take an intermediate approach and judge a loan applicant on the basis of both subjective and objective measures.

Character. From a lender's standpoint character is a measure of the importance a potential borrower attaches to meeting his or her obligations, especially those of a financial nature. Any lender would hope to attract borrowers who will make every effort to repay their loans. A lender may make a character judgment primarily on subjective factors, such as your appearance and personal manner at the time you apply for a loan. A lender may also place a great deal of importance on the comments of references you are able to supply. Lenders are likely to put great stock in the opinion of lenders who have had previous dealings with you.

Character is also judged by more objective criteria. The extent to which you have fulfilled previous loan commitments is likely to be a key consideration when a lender evaluates your character. A series of previous loan defaults will almost certainly be viewed as a serious character flaw for someone who is attempting to borrow money. The better able you are to convince a potential lender that you are a person who cares about your obligations and that you can

Credit bureaus are required to investigate items in your credit file that you dispute unless the dispute is judged as frivolous.

be trusted with someone else's money, the more likely the character issue will come down in your favor.

Capacity for repayment. The amount of cash flow you have available to help meet the terms of a loan is a significant consideration for any creditor. The larger your income relative to your expenses and existing loan payments, the greater your capacity to make the required payments on an additional loan. You have substantial capacity to make the payments on a new loan if you have considerable income, modest expenses, and few loan obligations. The stability of your income and the security of your employment are both important considerations for a lender, especially when you are requesting money for a relatively long period of time. In general, the more stable your income, in terms of both the amount and the source, the greater your capacity to meet a debt obligation.

Collateral. The collateral you are able to pledge on a loan helps ensure a lender against loss in the event you are unable to make required payments on a loan. Sufficient collateral can often overcome other deficiencies in your loan application. Even though your character is suspect and your income is barely adequate relative to the size of the loan you are seeking, substantial assets to pledge as collateral can help assure a lender that no money will be lost on a loan. The greater the value and liquidity of the assets (i.e., liquid assets can, by definition, be easily sold at market value) you are able to pledge as collateral, the more likely your loan application is to be approved.

Financial assets you own. The more financial assets you own free and clear of debt (i.e., assets that are not pledged as collateral against other loans), the greater a lender's confidence that you will be able to honor the terms of a loan.

Figure 12

BUILDING A GOOD CREDIT HISTORY

Individuals without a credit history often have difficulty obtaining credit. The Federal Trade Commission recommends several methods for building a good credit history:

- Open a checking account, a savings account, or both. Having accounts in your own name provides some evidence that you know how to manage money.
- Apply for a department store charge card. These are generally easier to obtain than national cards such as Visa, but using department store cards allows you to build a credit record.
- Ask someone to cosign your credit application. A cosigner will allow you to use someone else's credit history to build your own credit history.
- Ask if a financial institution will issue you a credit card using your savings account as collateral. This arrangement will keep you from having full access to your savings until you qualify for credit without collateral.
- If you are turned down for credit, find out why and attempt to clear up any mistakes.

Suppose you are interested in purchasing a new automobile. You own substantial amounts of CDs, common stocks, and bonds that could be sold to raise the funds you need, but there may be reasons you would rather retain the securities and seek funds from a lender. For example, there may be penalties or taxes you would have to pay on a sale. A lender is likely to view your assets as a reservoir that you can tap in the event your regular income or cash flow creates a problem in repaying a loan.

The Importance of Your Credit File

Individual credit histories are of interest to enough parties that entrepreneurs have formed companies to collect and distribute information about individual credit dealings. Privately operated credit bureaus collect and maintain personal and credit information about millions of individuals, probably including yourself. Each month thousands of bureaus collect, record, and transmit information to one or more of the country's three major credit bureaus.

Your credit file that is maintained at one or more credit bureaus contains personal information—including your name, current and former addresses, spouse, Social Security number, birthdate, current and past employers, and whether you rent or own your residence—and financial information—including your income, checks that have been returned for insufficient funds, and a detailed record of your past credit dealings. The credit record is likely to include the lending institution, loan amount, payment terms, and repayment history for each of your current and past loans. Credit files also contain legal information (e.g., bankruptcies and judgments) that appears in public notices.

> Contact your creditors in the event you are having difficulty meeting your loan payments. Many lenders are willing to restructure your payments in order to allow you to fully repay a loan.

Credit bureaus are actually nothing more than clearinghouses that collect and share credit information among creditors and other interested parties. Credit bureaus don't make a decision on your loan application. Rather, they supply information to members who make their own judgment. Lenders are at once the primary users of credit bureau information and the suppliers of most of the data contained in credit bureau files. Creditors utilize credit bureaus to check on the accuracy of information provided by loan applicants (are you really employed by Howell Brothers Car Care?) and to determine if applicants have honored current and past credit agreements. Employers who wish to check on applicants for employment find credit bureaus a valuable source of information.

Errors in Your Credit Report

Erroneous negative information that is part of your credit report can create major roadblocks to gaining credit or employment. There is ample opportunity for errors to creep into any system that involves daily postings and transfers of millions of pieces of information among millions of accounts. Credit data are sometimes posted to the wrong account, most frequently the account of someone who has an identical or similar name. Errors can occur when you use slightly different names (e.g., sometimes with your middle initial, sometimes without) to apply for credit.

In a credit file personal information such as income and employment is often outdated because it is typically entered only at the time you apply for credit, which may have last occurred several years ago. Confusion about some past transaction or credit relationship may cause faulty information to be part of your file. Perhaps a dispute with a creditor was eventually resolved, but the outcome escaped being posted in your account. An inquiry into the accuracy of credit information by a national consumer group found that nearly 20 percent of more than 150 credit files contained at least one error that was judged serious enough that it could result in denial of credit.

Correcting Errors in Your Credit File

Incorrect information in your credit file can cause you big headaches. Of course, correct information that puts you in a bad light can also cause difficulties. Most negative information remains in your file for seven years, and bankruptcy information may be retained for ten years. Without intervention on your part, incorrect negative information in your credit file spells long-term trouble for your dealings with potential employers and lenders.

Financial experts recommend that, every three or four years and at least six months prior to applying for a major loan, you should examine the information in your credit files at all three of the national credit bureaus noted in Figure 13. Allow adequate time to discover *and clear up* any errors. The clearing-up part can sometimes require more time than you expect. When sending for a copy of your credit file, request a brochure that outlines your legal rights with respect to the actions you may take.

> Debt collectors are not legally permitted to harass, oppress, or abuse you. You are permitted to sue debt collectors who violate this law.

Figure 13

THE THREE MAJOR CREDIT BUREAUS

- Equifax, P.O. Box 740241, Atlanta, GA 30374 (800-685-1111).
- Trans Union Credit Information Company, P.O. Box 3307, Tampa, FL 33601 (312–431–5100).
- TRW, National Consumer Assistance Center, P.O. Box 749029, Dallas, TX 75374 (800–226–1828). Requests for a complimentary credit report should be sent to TRW Complimentary Credit Report Request, P.O. Box 2350, Chatsworth, CA 91313-2350.

You have a legal right to know what is in your credit file, although you may have to pay a small fee to obtain a copy of the contents. TRW permits individuals one free copy per calendar year. You have a right to view the contents of your credit file without charge in the event you have been denied credit because of information contained in the file. To obtain the free copy, you must present a written request within thirty days of being denied credit. Contact the credit bureaus by using the information in Figure 13.

In the event you discover information in your file that you wish to dispute or have purged, what action should you take? First, you should complete and return the form that will be included in your file along with any supporting documentation you may have. For example, you may have a statement from a creditor indicating that you have successfully repaid a loan, whereas your credit report indicates that payments on the loan are behind schedule. If your credit file mistakenly contains information concerning someone else's financial dealings, you should contact both the credit bureau and the lender. The lender should have the borrower's Social Security number on file. Be certain to clearly and concisely explain your side of the dispute. Credit bureaus are required to undertake an investigation when they receive claims that their information is inaccurate or incomplete.

You have the right to include in your credit file a letter, of up to one hundred words, explaining your side of the dispute. You may also find it useful to include a letter that addresses a negative item that is not in dispute. For example, you might want your file to include a note explaining why you fell behind on repaying a loan (e.g., you were in the hospital, caring for your sick parents, or out of work). In the event you are unable to reach an acceptable resolution of your dispute, appeal directly to the creditor or other source of the negative information to provide a letter or some other written material that supports your side of the disagreement.

Credit Scoring

Although the information contained in your credit file is important, it is the lender, not the credit bureau, that will approve or disapprove your application for a loan. Lenders often reach decisions on credit applications by utilizing a

For a list of free publications about personal credit, write Public Reference, Room 130, Federal Trade Commission, Washington, DC 20580, and request a copy of *Best Sellers*.

Figure 14

FEDERAL CREDIT LAWS

The Equal Credit Opportunity Act Prohibits the denial of credit because of sex, race, marital status, religion, national origin, or age, or because the applicant receives public assistance.

The Fair Credit Billing Act Establishes procedures for resolving billing errors on credit card accounts.

The Fair Credit Reporting Act Gives creditors the right to learn what information is being distributed about them by credit bureaus.

The Fair Debt Collection Practices Act Prohibits debt collectors from using unfair or deceptive practices to collect overdue bills a creditor has forwarded for collection.

The Truth in Lending Act Requires lenders to provide borrowers with written disclosures of the cost of credit and the terms of repayment before borrowers enter into credit transactions.

The Federal Trade Commission is charged with enforcing these laws. Free brochures on these laws are available by writing Public Reference, Federal Trade Commission, Washington, DC 20580.

grading system that evaluates information contained in credit bureau reports in addition to information provided on loan applications. A loan applicant receives assigned points based on various factors, such as the length of time spent at the same address, age, length of tenure in the same job, amount of annual income, and number of dependents. High scores identify applicants who are expected to be good credit risks and who will be automatically approved for credit. Applicants with scores that fall in a medium range may require further evaluation or be approved for a nominal amount of credit. A low score will generally doom an applicant to seek another lender.

The components included in credit scoring systems and the relative importance of each component vary from lender to lender depending on what factors a particular lender feels are critical in identifying good credit risks. Individual factors such as job longevity and age are judged in relative importance according to how accurately the factors have tracked past loan performance. One lender may consider age to be only marginally useful in determining whether a borrower will successfully repay a loan, while another lender's experience may judge age to be an essential factor. Somewhat surprisingly, lenders are often more willing to grant you credit when you already have access to substantial amounts of credit through holding several credit cards.

Things to Take Care of Before You Apply for Credit

Several actions can be taken to improve your chances of success in obtaining a loan. Remember, it is to your advantage to make yourself into as attractive a loan applicant as possible. Your goal is to convince a lender that you will successfully repay the loan you are seeking.

> Under the Equal Credit Opportunity Act, reports to credit bureaus must be made in the names of both husband and wife if both use an account or are responsible for repaying the debt.

1. *Review your credit file.* The importance of this cannot be stressed too much. If your credit file contains negative information that is incorrect, you need to take action to have this information removed or corrected. If your file contains negative information that is not in dispute (i.e., you actually did mess up), provide a written explanation and have it included in your file. You have a legal right to do this.
2. *Prepare personal financial statements.* By now you should know that lenders will consider your loan request only after they have reviewed information concerning your income and debts. Some of the information will be obtained from your credit report. It will be to your advantage to assemble this information along with estimates of your expenses and assets so that you can present it to potential lenders at the time you apply for a loan. The task of assembling this financial information allows you to update your own knowledge of your financial status before meeting with a lender. This information will allow you to better support your loan application. The financial statements, even though they may be rudimentary, combined with financial awareness are likely to impress a lender and give you some leverage to bargain for better terms (e.g., a lower interest rate and/or a more favorable repayment schedule).

> Married females can choose to apply for credit in their first name and maiden name, their first name and their husband's last name, or a combined last name.

At the least, you should determine your current income and rough out an estimate of your major expenses (rent or mortgage payment, auto loan payment, utilities, insurance premiums, etc.). Also, put together a list of your major assets (car, home, furniture, etc.) along with a listing of the balances and required payments on each of your outstanding loans. This is information any creditor will eventually want to see, and you may as well become familiar with it before meeting with a lender.

CHAPTER 5

Managing Your Credit

Intelligent credit management means that you know when to borrow, how much to borrow, and where to borrow. You are able to choose the best mix of credit with respect to loan maturity, variable versus fixed interest rates, and payment size and frequency. You are able to handle your required loan payments without great strain and you have a plan for repaying your indebtedness. The ability to handle credit is influenced by many factors, including your current and future income, your current and future expenses, the interest rate you must pay on borrowed money, the payment terms on your outstanding loans, and, perhaps most important, your financial discipline.

Good credit management will lead to a more enjoyable life, eventually. You will spend money more wisely, keep your borrowing under control, save on the interest you pay to creditors, and sleep without worrying about how you are going to make next week's loan payment. If this sounds like some magic potion, don't be fooled. The benefits of credit management require a certain amount of sacrifice. You will probably find it necessary to eliminate, reduce, or delay some purchases you would ordinarily make, because a credit management program places limits on your borrowing. The major sacrifice of a credit management program is the purchases you will probably have to forgo, at least in the short run. Fortunately, in the long run you should be able to obtain more of the things you *really* want.

Determining Your Debt Limit

The ability to handle debt is primarily a function of the income that is available to make payments to lenders. This is the income that remains after you have met other required and basic spending needs, including taxes, insurance, retirement, food, shelter, and clothing. Although some flexibility probably exists for what you spend in each of these categories (other than taxes), there is a limit to your ability to reduce this spending. The greater the amount of current and projected income that remains after your required spending is taken care of, the larger the debt payments you should be able to handle without becoming financially strapped. Being able to handle larger debt payments means you can safely borrow additional money.

Required spending needs depend on many factors that,

Figure 15

ARE YOU OVEREXTENDED?

Some financial advisers suggest a rule-of-thumb measure to determine if you have taken on too much debt. Compare the percentage of your take-home pay (also called *disposable income*) that is required to service debts other than a home mortgage and credit card debt that is regularly paid in full. Then use the following chart to determine whether you have borrowed up to the maximum or have the capacity to borrow additional money.

Debt Payments as Percentage of Disposable Income	Debt Evaluation
10% or less	Debt is within safe limits
11% to 20%	Debt is being used to the maximum
More than 20%	You are overextended

in combination, are unique to your particular situation. Even something as basic as your state of residence plays a role in determining your spending requirements, because of differences in living costs and differences in taxes levied by the various states. Even more important are your family situation and lifestyle. A family with several children spends more money than an individual for most basic consumption items. Thus, an individual who is free of family obligations is generally able to support substantially more debt than a family that earns the same income.

Perhaps a simple example will serve to illustrate the relationship between income, required spending, and the capacity to handle debt. Suppose you are considering a $3,000 loan to help pay for the restoration of a classic automobile (read that as *junker)* you recently purchased. You would like to borrow the money now so that you can begin work on the car; you don't want, however, to take on a loan that will strap you financially. Your current take-home pay is $2,000 per month after taxes, Social Security, health insurance, and your retirement contribution have been deducted from gross income. You estimate that you spend approximately $1,200 each month for rent, utilities, food, insurance (other than health), and clothing, which leaves $800 to support debt payments and other spending needs. This amount should prove adequate to service the payments on a $3,000 loan, even if repayment is to be made within one or two years. A two-year loan at 9 percent annual interest would require twenty-four monthly payments of $137 each. On the other hand, if your take-home pay is regularly depleted by the end of each month, you are in poor shape to take on a debt obligation unless you have the financial discipline to reduce your other spending.

> The most you will have to pay for unauthorized charges on a lost or stolen credit card is $50, even though someone has charged hundreds of dollars worth of merchandise before you report the card missing. You are not required to pay for any unauthorized charges made after you notify the card issuer of the loss of your card.

Figure 16

SIGNS OF TOO MUCH DEBT

- You pay the minimum required payment on your credit cards.
- You borrow to make the required payments on your existing debt.
- You are missing payments to your creditors.
- The balances on your credit cards are increasing each month.
- Payments to creditors take such a large proportion of your income that there is little left over for necessities.
- You have to find extra work in order to meet your bills.
- You have gotten into the habit of raiding your savings in order to meet your monthly expenses.
- You don't expect to be able to repay your creditors.

The Importance of Maintaining a Personal Budget

Most individuals and families can derive substantial benefits from maintaining a personal budgeting system. The less income you have left at the end of any month and the more you wonder where your money went, the more you will benefit from a personal budget. From the standpoint of credit management, a budget allows you to determine your credit needs and to evaluate your ability to handle credit. The financial planning required to maintain a budget makes it less likely that you will fall into the trap of borrowing to satisfy your immediate needs without first considering how this borrowing will affect your ability to take care of future needs. Keep in mind that most loans represent borrowing from the future to satisfy present needs. Financial planning is the key to controlling this borrowing with good credit management.

Developing a Personal Budget

A personal budget requires that you develop a forecast for your expected income and expenditures for the length of the budget (e.g., one year, two years, five years, or however long you decide is necessary). The forecast periods in a personal budget are typically set at the same interval as your pay: weekly forecasts if you are paid weekly, and monthly forecasts if you are paid monthly. Comparing your income and spending forecasts allows you to judge whether your expected income will support all your planned expenditures. A forecast that indicates planned expenditures will exceed expected income alerts you to a need to reduce your planned expenditures, draw on your savings, or borrow. You can decide which of these options is best suited to your particular circumstances.

Estimating your income. Estimating your weekly or monthly income generally presents few problems, especially if you earn a salary or receive a pension that remains the same from one pay period to the next. Income is more difficult to forecast when you are paid an hourly wage for a job that has uncertain hours. A typical workweek that varies between twenty and fifty hours makes it difficult to forecast how much you will be making next month, let alone your income during the same period next year.

The income portion of your budget should include the earnings of your spouse and income from savings accounts and other investments you may have. If you use gross income (your total salary or wage) for the budgeted earnings, be certain that all your payroll deductions (withholding for federal and state taxes, Social Security, health insurance, etc.) are included in the expenditures section of the budget. An alternative method is to use your net pay, or take-home pay (i.e., the net amount of your paycheck after payroll deductions) which allows you to avoid dealing with payroll deductions.

Estimating your expenses. Personal expenses tend to be difficult to forecast, especially if you haven't been paying much attention to how your income is being spent. Expenses are difficult to estimate partly because there are so many categories and subcategories of spending—groceries, medicines, restaurant meals, electricity, and on and on. Do you spend money on fifty different items per week? a hundred? You probably don't have a clue. The great variety of expenditures makes it difficult to keep track of your current spending and to estimate your future spending.

The considerable monthly variation in many categories of spending is another reason expenses are difficult to forecast. Think how much your monthly electric bill varies from month to month, and from the corresponding month last year. How about spending on clothing? Prices of many food items are very volatile and especially difficult to forecast.

> You are entering the financial trouble zone when you find yourself borrowing money in order to be able to pay off the balance on another loan that has come due. When you have difficulty making loan payments with your current income, you have become overextended.

The first step in estimating your monthly expenditures over the next year or two (or more) is to compile a fairly detailed record of your past spending patterns. Even though you haven't saved the receipts for all the goods and services you have purchased during the past several years, you probably have credit card statements and check registers that will provide much of the data you need to reconstruct your spending. The total amount of your weekly or monthly spending can be estimated by subtracting the amount you have saved each period from the income you earned in the period. Keep in mind that some bills are paid later, so this method provides only an estimate, not an exact amount of spending.

Major expenditures are often fairly easy to estimate: The rent or mortgage payment, the automobile loan payment, insurance premiums, and several utility bills remain relatively constant from one period to the next. It is more difficult to develop a spending forecast for groceries, restaurant meals, clothing, and other types of spending that fluctuate from period to period. Still, an examination of your past spending patterns is a great help for estimating how you are likely to be spending your future income.

Summary of income and spending estimates. Each period's forecast for total income and total spending provides an advance look at whether you are likely to experience a surplus or a shortage of money during a particular budgeting interval. You can expect to be able to add to your savings, prepay some debt, or increase spending above planned levels during periods when the forecast indicates that income will exceed spending. If the excess proves to be unusually large you may be able to accomplish all three goals. On the other hand, you are likely to have to draw on your sav-

Figure 17

OUTLINE OF A PERSONAL BUDGET

	January	February	March
Income Projections			
Salary			
Spouse salary			
Interest from savings			
Dividends	_____	_____	_____
Total income			
Spending Projections			
Rent			
Groceries			
Clothing			
Utilities			
Life insurance			
Auto insurance			
Entertainment			
Miscellaneous	_____	_____	_____
Total spending			
Surplus or Deficit (income less spending)			

ings, borrow, or reduce spending below planned levels during periods when your expenditures are forecasted to exceed your income.

Large, occasional expenses such as tax payments and insurance premiums might cause you to project deficits during several months each year. Occasional deficits are not particularly worrisome if they are offset by expected surpluses during other months. Ideally, your spending plans could be revised to reduce or postpone certain expenditures during the months when deficits are anticipated. Another, less desirable option, is to plan to take out a short-term loan during the deficit months.

A forecast showing planned spending will regularly exceed expected income is cause for genuine concern. Forecasts of continuing deficits call for major reductions in your spending plans (or a quick change of employment) unless you have accumulated a substantial stash of money that can be used to offset the planned deficits. If you are unable or unwilling to plan now for the changes that will bring your budget into balance (i.e., make your spending and income approximately equal), unwelcome changes will eventually be forced upon you when little maneuvering room is available.

How a Personal Budget Improves Credit Management

A budget accounts for both cash and credit purchases, but in very different ways. Forecasts for cash transactions are entered in the budgeting period in which the respective purchases are expected to occur. If you anticipate spending $200 per month on groceries, enter $200 on the appropriate line for each of the months your budget covers. If you expect that grocery prices will increase by 10 percent during the coming year, add an additional $20 per month to next year's monthly budgeting periods.

How to Account for Credit Purchases in a Personal Budget

Credit purchases should not be entered in the expenditures section of your personal budget. Rather, you should enter only the payment or payments that you expect to be making to the lenders that financed the credit purchases. If you purchase a new car with the proceeds of a dealer loan, your budget should show the monthly payments required by the loan agreement, and not the purchase price of the car. The price paid for the car does not represent a cash expenditure unless you pay in cash at the time of the purchase. Any down payment required by a lender will be included in your budget during the month the down payment is to be made.

Do not make the mistake of counting a credit purchase twice; once when the purchase is to occur and again when you expect to repay the loan that financed the purchase. A personal budget includes cash income and cash expenses, and the only cash expenses relevant to a credit purchase are the down payment (if applicable) and the payments on the loan that financed the purchase. If you purchase a new home with the proceeds of a loan, the payments required to repay the loan, rather than the purchase price of the house, are entered in the expenditures section of your personal budget.

> If you are a good money manager who prefers to take care of things ahead of time, try to avoid having prepayment penalties included in your loan contract. You don't want to have to pay a penalty in the event you find yourself with some extra funds that can be used to pay down a loan and reduce your interest expense.

Suppose that eighteen months ago, you used the proceeds of a four-year loan to purchase a new car. The loan was scheduled to be repaid with forty-eight monthly payments of $280, and thirty payments remain before the loan is fully repaid. The loan obligation resulting from the credit purchase should be included in your budget by listing a $280 expenditure for each of the next thirty months (see Figure 18). This assumes, of course, that you expect to keep the car until the loan is completely repaid. If you intend to continue driving the current car beyond the last scheduled loan payment, entries for the loan will fall to zero beyond thirty months, when loan payments cease. Continuing to drive a car beyond the date of the last loan payment does wonders for your personal budget. If you anticipate trading cars before the current loan is repaid, replace the $280 entry with a new, higher payment (you will need to estimate a payment amount based on the cost of the car you intend to purchase) beginning in the month you expect to trade.

Accounting for Multiple Loans

Individuals and families frequently find themselves being required to make payments on several loans at one time. It is not unusual for a family to have a mortgage on their home, one or two car loans, a home-equity loan, and outstanding balances on one or more credit cards. New loans are periodically taken out at the same time that balances on existing loans are being reduced. With several outstanding loans you end up managing a "loan portfolio" that is continuously being reduced and increased as existing loans are paid off and new loans are added. The ability to take on the responsibility of new debt payments is partly determined by suc-

Figure 18

PERSONAL BUDGET WITH LOAN PAYMENT ADDED

	January	February	March
Income Projections			
Salary			
Spouse salary			
Interest from savings			
Dividends	______	______	______
Total Income			
Spending Projections			
Rent			
Groceries			
Clothing			
Utilities			
Life insurance			
Auto insurance			
Entertainment			
Miscellaneous	______	______	______
Total spending			
Loan Payments			
Surplus or Deficit (Income less spending less loan payments)			

cess at repaying existing loans. You can feel comfortable purchasing a new automobile with borrowed money only when you have completely repaid the loan you made several years ago to pay for a bathroom remodeling.

If you have several outstanding loans and expect to undertake additional borrowing during the time horizon covered by your budgeting system, payments associated with each loan should be entered on a separate line of your budget as shown in Figure 19. The payments required by your home mortgage are listed on one line, payments for your auto loan are listed on a separate line, and so forth. Using separate lines for each set of loan payments makes it easier to identify the budgeting impact of each outstanding loan. While lumping together all your loan payments into a single monthly entry does permit you to determine if your total debt obligations, combined with other projected expenses, will exceed your projected income, it doesn't allow you to identify the particular loans that are the primary cause of this problem.

Interpreting Budget Information Concerning Your Debts

A personal budget helps you manage your credit by allowing you to determine the total amount of debt payments you can handle during any particular time period. Knowing the upper limit of the loan payments you will be able to make may be effective in controlling your borrowing. Being forced

> Don't pay extra for a credit card that offers perks you are unlikely to use. This may mean you should choose a regular card over a more expensive gold card.

Figure 19

MULTIPLE LOAN ENTRIES IN A PERSONAL BUDGET

	January	February	March
Loan Payments			
Mortgage	$750	$750	$750
Auto loan (Chevrolet)	420	420	
Auto loan (Jeep)			380
Credit union (personal loan)	120	120	
Total payments	$1,290	$1,290	$1,130

This example assumes that the loan on the Chevrolet is fully paid off in February, at which time money is borrowed to purchase the Jeep. The credit union loan is fully repaid in February, so no payment is necessary in March.

to come to grips with the spending you will have to give up in order to meet the payments on a loan is another factor that is likely to dampen your demand for credit. A personal budget forces you to consider the other expenditures you must forgo in order to make the required payments on a loan. Economists call this trade-off opportunity cost. The opportunity cost of taking out a loan weighs purchases you are unable to make against the loan payments.

Suppose you are debating whether to trade cars in several months. The car you want to purchase is relatively expensive, and the payments on a new four-year loan will run $520 per month, a substantial increase over the $280 you are paying on your current loan. To determine whether you can afford to trade cars and incur additional debt, rework your budget expenditure projections by substituting a $520 loan payment for the current $280 payment, beginning three months from the current month. The loan payments section of your personal budget will now include three monthly entries of $280 and subsequent monthly entries of $520.

The higher loan payment resulting from trading automobiles will cause no great financial strain if your budget has been projecting substantial surpluses. Incorporating the higher loan payments into your revised budget projections should indicate a continuation of a surplus, although at a reduced level. This indicates that you should be able to handle the additional debt that results from trading cars. On the other hand, if you are currently forecasting several years of balanced budgets, an increased loan payment may cause a shift from a series of small monthly surpluses and deficits to a series of substantial monthly deficits.

What are your options when budget projections indicate you will be facing extended monthly deficits? Doing nothing will cause you to draw on your savings (if sufficient funds are available) or to borrow additional money in order to be able to make your car payments. The borrowing option

> Make it a point to pay off your most expensive debt first. Generally, this means keeping credit card balances as close to zero as possible. It doesn't make sense to pay ahead on an 8-percent home mortgage with tax-deductible interest when you have outstanding credit card balances running up interest at a rate of 14 to 18 percent.

Figure 20

POSSIBLE COURSES OF ACTION WHEN FORECASTED EXPENDITURES EXCEED EXPECTED INCOME

- Increase your income by working more hours or locating a better-paying job.
- Reduce planned spending in one or more budget categories.
- Refinance one or more loans to lengthen the maturities and reduce the amount of the monthly payments.
- Draw on your savings.
- Borrow.
- Sell assets you own.

means you will be taking out a loan for the purpose of helping you pay an existing loan. This is a poor choice, because it means you are putting off a needed restructuring of your spending plans.

One obvious solution to an expected budget deficit is to forgo the new car and continue driving your current vehicle. You might also consider purchasing a smaller car or a less costly used car that will allow you to borrow less money. You can also investigate the possibility of financing the new car for five years rather than four years. Extending the period of the loan for an additional year will reduce the amount of your monthly payments. Unfortunately, a loan with a longer maturity prolongs the agony of making payments and restricts your other spending for a longer period. An extended maturity also causes you to incur greater interest expenses over the life of the loan. Another course of action is to plunge ahead with the trade and plan to reduce other spending, something that is often easier said than done. It is one thing to rationalize that you will cut back on spending for utilities and groceries in future months, but it is something else again to actually do the cutting.

Personal Bankruptcy: The Last Resort

Personal bankruptcy is a last-ditch solution that erects a legal barrier between you and your creditors while you attempt to sort out the dreary state of your finances. Bankruptcy isn't a no-cost solution, because you are likely to be forced to part with some of your assets before the process is complete. On the other hand, a bankruptcy filing won't require you to give up everything you own. Your home, a vehicle that provides transportation to work, clothing, and certain other assets can often be retained in a personal bankruptcy proceeding. The particular assets you are legally able to keep depend in large part on the law of the state in which you reside.

Another important consideration is that bankruptcy will leave a blot on your financial record that is likely to cause creditors to give you a wide berth for quite some time. Financial institutions often view a bankruptcy as proof that you are a poor money manager who chose to renege on your promises to creditors. Why should they expect something different in the future? Creditors will be aware of a bankruptcy filing through your credit file, where the information will remain for up to ten years.

The bankruptcy route to financial rescue was once re-

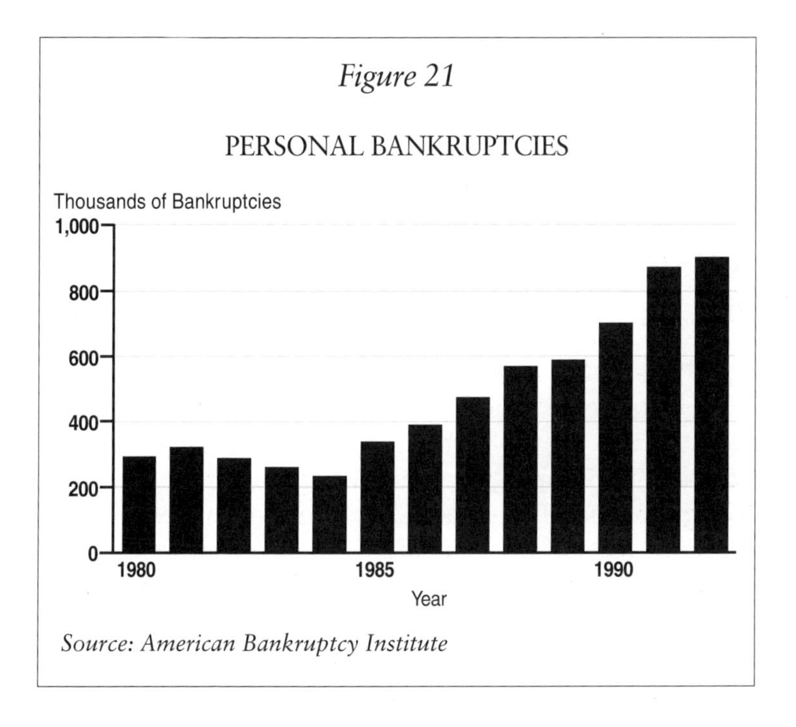

Figure 21

PERSONAL BANKRUPTCIES

Source: American Bankruptcy Institute

served for individuals in desperate financial condition who were willing to endure the scorn of friends, relatives, associates, creditors, and nearly anyone else who learned of the bankruptcy filing. How times have changed. Today, bankruptcy is considered by many to be an acceptable step for persons who are unable or unwilling to live up to their financial commitments, even though this escape hatch is often abused by individuals who borrow large amounts of money with no intention of making repayment. Although your friends and neighbors may not harbor ill will because of your bankruptcy (at least, not outwardly), you are likely to find that creditors have a long memory.

Although personal bankruptcy should be a last resort when you are facing financial problems, there comes a point when you can become so mired in debt that there is no possibility for escape because creditors are clamoring for virtually all of your income. You may experience a serious illness and be subject to medical bills so large that there is no possibility you can ever fully repay your creditors. Likewise, a major legal judgment resulting from an accident you cause may force you to consider bankruptcy.

A bankruptcy filing keeps most creditors at bay until you are able to arrange some type of debt repayment plan that is acceptable to all the parties. The repayment plan can include an extension of your debts (i.e., smaller payments over a longer period of time), a reduction in the interest charges you must pay, or a reduction in the amount of the debt. A bankruptcy filing does not affect your responsibility for child support, alimony, and certain types of taxes. Most experts strongly suggest that you seek help from an attorney (who is likely to require a cash down payment or, perhaps, payment in full) before filing your bankruptcy petition. You may find that you can negotiate a debt restructuring with your creditors without actually filing for bankruptcy. Many creditors find mention of bankruptcy to be sufficiently threatening (they often have a lot to lose) that they will renegotiate the terms of a loan rather than face the uncertain outcome of a bankruptcy.

> Make it a goal to be free of debt by the time you retire. Even if this is unrealistic, make an effort to reduce the amount you owe as you near retirement. You don't want to face retirement with major debts hanging over you.

Figure 22

TWO TYPES OF PERSONAL BANKRUPTCY

Individuals or families typically file for bankruptcy because of large medical expenses, job loss, divorce, or credit abuse. In the event you become mired in debt and your creditors are uncooperative in agreeing to restructure your loans, bankruptcy may prove to be the only feasible alternative. Actually, two types of personal bankruptcy are available, Chapter 7 and Chapter 13.

Chapter 7 Bankruptcy

- You must file a petition with the bankruptcy court that lists all your assets and debts. The filing fee is currently about $200.
- You may file a bankruptcy petition without the assistance of an attorney.
- You will be required to sell all of your assets that are not specifically protected under state law.
- State laws generally permit you to retain a home, clothing, tools of your trade, and a means of transportation. There is a limit on the value of each of these.
- Your creditors are likely to have to accept less than full repayment of their loans.
- Following the bankruptcy you have no additional obligations to your creditors.
- Certain debts, such as tax obligations, alimony, child support, and student loans, cannot be settled in bankruptcy court.
- This type of bankruptcy can be used only one time every six years.

Chapter 13 Bankruptcy

- A court-appointed trustee uses your future earnings to repay your creditors.
- The repayment can occur over a three- to five-year period.
- Your creditors are likely to have to settle for only partial repayment of your debts.
- You are required to have legal representation to file.
- You are permitted to retain your assets.

In truth, creditors often play an important role in personal credit difficulties. Overly aggressive merchants convince people to buy things they can't afford (merchants often don't know or care what their customers can afford), and aggressive creditors allow people to borrow more money than they can reasonably be expected to repay. Personal bankruptcies caused by overspending and excess borrowing return to haunt creditors, who then may receive only partial repayment on their outstanding loans.

CHAPTER 6

Credit Cards

Credit cards can provide financial flexibility and freedom. Carrying one or more cards provides you with substantial amounts of purchasing power without being required to lug around large amounts of cash. Credit card benefits are greatest for consumers who are able to escape finance charges by paying the entire amount of their outstanding balances each month. Unfortunately, too much of a good thing often becomes a bad thing. Purchases using credit cards are convenient, sometimes too much so, thereby causing many cardholders to overspend and overcharge. Card issuers charge relatively high interest rates on unpaid credit card balances, causing a major drain on the purchasing power of consumers who remain perpetually in hock to the card companies.

Credit cards and their close relatives, automated teller machine (ATM) cards, debit cards, travel and entertainment (T&E) cards, and charge cards, are fast becoming the preferred method of payment for many types of transactions. For years people have used these cards to pay for travel-related purchases, such as gasoline, lodging, airplane and rail tickets, and restaurant meals. More recently credit cards have gained popularity for buying personal items that in years past were typically purchased with cash or by check. Credit cards have become virtually a necessity when ordering merchandise via telephone. Increasingly, credit, debit, and ATM cards are used to obtain cash from ATMs that remain open around the clock, rain or shine, 365 days per year.

The new uses and wider acceptance of plastic money have caused most individuals to consider it a necessity to carry one or more credit cards. Some individuals have dozens of cards, many of which they seldom use. Have you attempted to rent a vehicle recently without having a credit card? How about checking into a hotel for a stay of several days? Have you noticed how long it takes to receive merchandise ordered by telephone when you choose to pay by check? Plastic is power, at least until the bills come due.

How the Cards Work

Credit cards, charge cards, debit cards, and T&E cards can be used to pay for purchases of goods and services at business establishments that accept the particular type of card you have. The cards are used as replacements for payment by cash or check. The merchant who accepts your card for

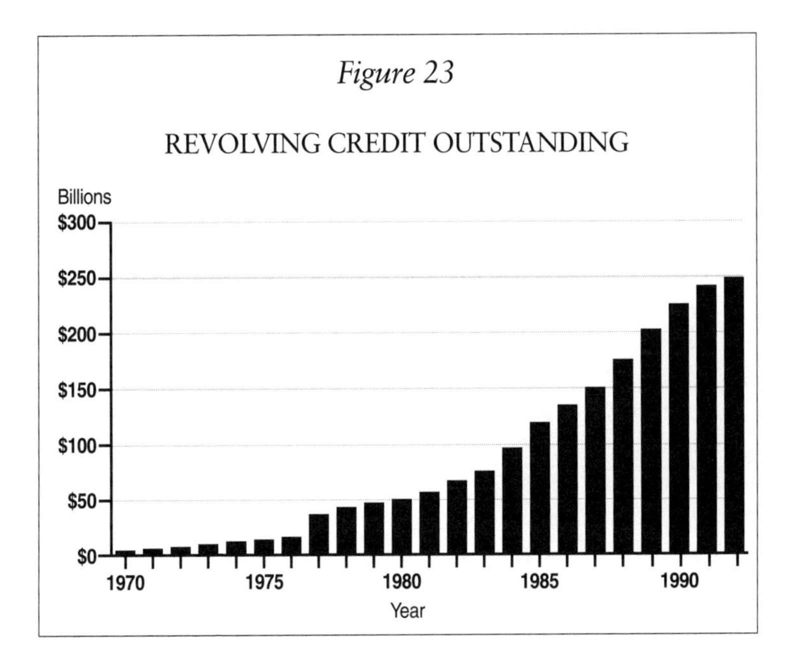

Figure 23

REVOLVING CREDIT OUTSTANDING

payment remits a copy of the signed receipt to a clearinghouse or to the card company, which then reimburses the merchant for 95 to 98 percent of the dollar amount that is submitted. The remaining 2 to 5 percent is kept by the card company as a service fee. The size of the fee depends on the merchant's type of business and the amount of charged purchases the merchant submits for reimbursement. Small merchants have the least negotiating power and generally pay the highest fees. These service fees are paid by the merchant, not by you (you may end up paying other fees), although some economists contend that merchants must cover these fees by raising the prices of the goods and services they sell. If this theory is correct, even consumers who choose to pay with cash end up paying higher prices when they buy goods and services from merchants who accept payment by credit card.

Some businesses accept several different cards for payment while other businesses are more selective and accept only one or two cards. For example, many merchants accept only Visa and MasterCard. Some retailers accept only their own card. If you make a purchase from a business that accepts Visa and its own card and you have only a MasterCard, too bad. You better have cash or a spare check. A large number of businesses do not accept payment by anything other than cash (or, in some cases, by check), primarily because they do not want to pay the service fees demanded by the card companies. At present few fast-food restaurants, grocery stores, or movie theaters accept payment by credit card. Many small businesses accept only cash or checks. You cannot use cards to pay bills, buy postage stamps, or to pay your taxes (although there have been proposals to change this). A business with no competitors has little incentive to accept cards for payment.

Types of Cards

While the term *credit card* is often used in a generic sense to identify any card that can be used for making purchases, the term more properly identifies a card that possesses certain characteristics. Actually, some cards frequently referred to as credit cards don't provide access to credit at all. You should understand the differences among different types of cards so that you will be able to make an informed choice regarding the type of card that is best for you.

The chances are that you can enjoy all the benefits provided by credit cards while holding a single national credit card. Having one card facilitates maintenance of records by keeping monthly statements and bills to a minimum. The fewer bills you receive, the less likely you are to forget to pay one of them.

Credit cards. Credit cards such as MasterCard, Visa, and Discover allow you to charge purchases or draw cash advances from financial institutions and ATMs. You can use a credit card as often as you like so long as the outstanding balance in your account does not exceed a predetermined maximum (your *credit line)* established by the card's issuer. You may want to request an increase in your credit line if you tend to make substantial credit purchases that regularly bump against the maximum. Credit card companies levy finance charges on accounts that are not paid in full by each statement's due date.

Some financial institutions issue *secured* credit cards—cards that carry a credit line equal to the amount of money you have on deposit at that institution. Funds in your account can be used to cover any bills you fail to pay. Secured cards are generally of interest only to individuals who have a poor credit history (or no credit history) and are unable to qualify for a regular credit card. An expanded discussion of credit cards follows this section.

Do not give your credit card number to anyone over the telephone unless you initiate the call. There are many unscrupulous callers who will offer good deals in exchange for your credit card number. The deals never materialize, but your credit card account is likely to end up with unauthorized charges.

Figure 24

THE PLASTIC TRAVELER'S CHECK

In late 1993, news stories reported that Visa USA was preparing to issue a prepaid travel card. Consumers would pay in advance for the card, which would be "encoded" with a specific amount of money. The card would be used in ATMs to obtain cash and in point-of-sale terminals to pay for purchases. Cards would be discarded when the encoded funds were depleted.

Companies issuing prepaid travel cards were expected to charge a fee similar to that charged for traveler's checks (i.e., a percentage of the amount of money encoded in the card). The card issuer would also benefit from the availability of extra funds between the time a card was purchased and the time the card was used to draw cash or pay for merchandise. Cardholders would benefit from having a safe source of cash and from being able to obtain foreign currencies at favorable exchange rates from ATMs around the world.

Debit cards. Debit cards, issued by many of the same financial institutions that issue credit cards, can be used to pay for purchases or to obtain cash advances, but the amount of a purchase is immediately deducted from your checking account at the financial institution that issued the card. Debit cards offer convenience (you don't have to carry cash or bother to write a check) but no credit—thus, the difference in names. Although generally offered without a fee, debit cards have failed to gain popularity with consumers because of the need to have funds available in order to use the cards. Using a debit card is a convenient method of writing a check.

T&E cards. T&E cards, such as American Express and Diners Club, can be used to pay for purchases from merchants that accept the cards. These cards are accepted at fewer establishments than credit cards. Unlike credit cards that allow you to carry unpaid balances into subsequent months, T&E accounts must be paid in full each month. Thus, T&E cards give you an extra thirty to fifty days before you are required to come up with money to pay for the purchases you charged, but they don't allow you to extend payment further, even with interest.

Charge cards. Charge cards can be used to purchase goods and services at the businesses issuing the cards. Petroleum companies and department stores (Sears, Roebuck and J. C. Penney) issue charge cards in part to build customer loyalty. Charge cards do not involve an annual fee and are generally easier to obtain than national credit cards. Other than the severe restriction on where these cards can be used, charge cards function much like credit cards. Cardholders who pay their monthly bill in full avoid finance charges. Partial payments result in unpaid balances that cause finance charges to be added. Charge cards have lost popularity as issuers of these cards increasingly accept national credit cards.

ATM cards. Like debit cards, ATM cards do not provide a user with access to credit. Rather, these cards allow you to make cash withdrawals from your checking account at thousands of ATMs around the world. ATM cards offer the

Always take and destroy any carbons from credit card receipts to make it more difficult for someone to steal your credit card number. Some newer receipt forms no longer utilize carbons.

convenience of being able to obtain cash at any time and at many locations, but they have nothing to do with credit. Thus, no more discussion of this subject.

Characteristics of Credit Cards

All credit cards convey similar benefits, but at differing costs to the cardholder. Credit card companies sometimes offer added benefits, such as travel insurance, travel discounts, and collision insurance for car rentals, to convince consumers to apply for and use their cards. Everybody is looking for an edge.

Cardholder Liability

In the event your credit card is lost, stolen, or used by someone else without proper authorization, you are responsible for charges to a maximum of $50 per card. Any liability on your part assumes that you have been previously informed of this liability (read the fine print). You will generally not be held responsible for any unauthorized use of your credit card if you immediately report a lost or stolen card by phoning a number listed on your statement. Your liability for unauthorized use of your *debit card* (if you have one) can be substantially larger than the liability for a credit card. The $50 liability limit applies to a debit card only if you re-

> You can avoid paying an annual fee for a credit card if you cancel the card in writing within forty days of when you first receive a bill for the fee.

port the loss of the card to the credit card company *within two business days of discovering the loss*. In the event you miss the two-day limit, you can be held responsible for up to $500 in unauthorized charges. You can be held for unlimited unauthorized use if you fail to notify the card company within sixty days of unauthorized charges appearing on your statement.

Charges to Cardholders

Credit cards are made available because they are expected to produce a profit for the financial institutions that issue them. In fact, these cards have become so profitable for many financial institutions that an increasing number of players including Sears, American Telephone & Telegraph, General Motors, and Ford Motor Company have entered the fray. Intense competition among card companies has produced some good deals for consumers, but you need to understand your own credit needs and know what things to look for in order to make a wise choice among the hundreds of cards that are available.

Annual fees. Some card companies charge cardholders an annual fee that typically ranges between $25 and $100. Issuers sometimes offer two classes of cards, a regular card and a premium card, with different annual fees. An annual fee is generally charged to a cardholder's account on the initial statement and on each subsequent renewal date. Credit card issuers that charge an annual fee will sometimes forgive or reduce the fee, but only if you ask. You are permitted to avoid paying the annual fee if, within thirty days of receiving the statement that includes the fee, you notify the card company that you wish to cancel your card.

Competition has caused many credit card companies to eliminate or reduce the annual fees they charge cardholders. The financial institutions that offer these cards haven't adjusted their fees to be good guys, but rather to attract new applicants and increase renewals among current cardholders, who regularly receive solicitations from competing financial institutions. A list of credit card companies that do not charge an annual fee appears in each weekly issue of *Barron's* and in each monthly issue of *Money.* Remember, credit card companies earn income from charges to merchants who accept the cards (i.e., discounts on reimbursements) as well as from fees charged to cardholders.

Other fees. Several miscellaneous fees are levied by many credit card companies, including some issuers that don't charge an annual fee. These fees need only be considered if they apply to your particular situation.

- Card companies sometimes charge a fee for issuing more than one card per account. This charge isn't important if you need only a single card, but it should become a consideration if you require additional cards for your spouse and college-age son.
- A penalty may be assessed if the outstanding balance in your account exceeds the credit limit you have been granted. Requesting a credit limit increase may help avoid this fee but also may leave you overextended.
- Card companies often levy a fee for cash advances. The fee may involve a flat charge of from $1.00 to $10.00 per transaction, or a percentage fee of from 1 to 5 percent of the money you obtain. Fees are sometimes different for cash advances obtained from inside a bank, compared with advances obtained from an ATM (you figure out why).

> Do not write your personal information number (PIN) on your credit card. Anyone finding your card and learning your PIN can use the card to withdraw cash from automated teller machines.

- You will generally be assessed a fee if you pay less than the required minimum payment or if you pay later than the due date indicated on your statement. The late fee is in addition to interest that is computed on your unpaid balance.

Finance Charges on Credit Card Accounts

Both interest rates and the method by which interest charges are calculated vary from one credit card company to the next. Fortunately, card companies must disclose the interest rate they charge, along with the method they use to calculate the finance charges that are added to your account.

Credit card companies typically allow a *grace period* of twenty-five or thirty days beyond the billing date, during which time you can avoid interest charges by paying the full balance of your account. If you are billed on January 5 by a credit card company that extends a twenty-five-day grace period, you have until January 30 to pay the full amount of the bill without incurring an interest charge. So long as you continue to pay each new monthly balance by the due date, you will not be required to pay any interest. A long grace period operates to your advantage because you have longer to pay your bill without having interest charges posted to your account. A few card companies offer no grace period, which means these companies begin charging interest as soon as credit purchases are posted to your account. You should make every effort to avoid using a credit card that provides no grace period for payments.

The High Cost of Credit Card Interest

In general, credit card companies charge relatively high rates of interest on unpaid balances. There is some justification for the high charges, since it is expensive to operate a credit card business. Consider the simplicity of making home loans in which a single loan for $100,000 or more will often remain in effect for fifteen or twenty years. The lender merely sits back and lets the checks roll in (unless, of course, the borrower quits paying). Compare this with a credit card operation in which huge numbers of charges and reimbursements—often for relatively small amounts of money—are required every day. Resolving the many cardholder complaints concerning improper charges, shoddy merchandise, late payments, lost cards, late receipt of statements, and so forth is an expensive proposition. And what about all of the money lost by card companies because of fraud and nonpayment by cardholders? Overextended cardholders flee to bankruptcy court or simply quit making payments. Thieves steal credit cards and credit card numbers to make purchases that are never paid.

The majority of credit card companies calculate interest using a fixed rate of interest that changes only infrequently. Even though short-term market rates of interest are constantly on the move, interest rates charged on most credit cards change by only small amounts, if at all. Interest charges on credit cards are usually quite high during weak economic periods when market rates are relatively low. During a period of very high market rates of interest, interest rates charged by credit card companies may actually seem reasonable.

Some financial institutions charge variable interest rates on credit card balances. The interest rate charged on the unpaid balances of these cards is generally equal to the prime rate (the interest rate that commercial banks charge their most creditworthy borrowers) plus 2 to 7 percent, depending on the policy of the particular card company. Cards with variable rates offer relatively low finance charges (compared with cards with fixed rates) during periods when market rates of interest are low, and the highest finance charges during periods when market rates of interest are high.

How Finance Charges Are Calculated

Credit card companies calculate the finance charges they add to monthly statements by applying a periodic interest rate to the outstanding balance in a cardholder's account. As we shall see, credit card companies use several methods for determining the balance in an account that is subject to interest charges. The periodic interest rate is calculated by dividing the annual percentage rate by the number of billing periods in a year, generally twelve. Thus, an annual percent-

> Credit card companies normally allow several days beyond the payment date listed on your statement for you to pay without incurring penalty or finance charges. Call or write the card issuer to determine the company's policy regarding the last day when payment can be *received* without penalty.

age rate of 15 percent converts to a periodic rate of 15 percent divided by twelve, or 1.25 percent per period when finance charges are calculated monthly. The periodic interest rate is multiplied by the appropriate balance to determine the dollar amount of the monthly finance charge.

The method used to calculate the balance in an account that is subject to interest charges is very important in determining the finance charges that will be added to the account. If you consistently pay your balance in full and on time you will not normally incur any finance charges unless the financial institution that issues your card does not permit a grace period. On the other hand, if you regularly carry outstanding balances on your card (i.e., you always owe money to the card company) and, as a result, incur finance charges every month, the method for computing your balance is crucial, because it can make a big difference in how much you will have to pay for credit.

Adjusted balance. The balance at the beginning of each billing cycle is adjusted downward for payments you made during the same cycle, but the balance is not adjusted for purchases you made during the cycle. The date the financial institution receives your payment does not affect the balance that is used for calculating finance charges so long as the payment is posted during the billing cycle. The adjusted balance method of calculating your outstanding balance is most favorable from your standpoint, because it results in the lowest finance charge.

Average daily balance. The balances in your account during each day of the billing cycle are added together, and the result is divided by the number of days in the cycle. In calculating the average daily balance, payments you make during the cycle are subtracted from the amount you owe. New credit purchases that are posted to your account during the cycle *may* be included in the calculation. Most, but not all, credit card companies include new credit purchases when calculating the finance charge for your account. It is to your advantage that the credit card company *not* include new purchases in calculating the balance subject to the periodic interest rate, because the resulting balance will be higher than if new purchases are excluded.

Two-cycle average daily balance. The balances in your account during each day of the *last two* billing cycles are added together, and the sum is divided by the number of days in the two billing cycles. The average daily balance is then multiplied by the periodic interest rate to determine the finance charge for the month. Payments you make during the two billing cycles are subtracted in calculating the average, but new purchases may or may not be added to the balance, depending on the credit card company's method of calculation.

Previous balance. The periodic interest rate is applied against the beginning balance of your account to determine the month's finance charge. No payments or credit purchases made during the month are included in the calculation.

Ending balance. The monthly finance charge is calculated by multiplying the periodic interest rate times the balance at the end of the billing period. The timing of

> Be certain you understand the fees and/or interest you will be charged on a credit card cash advance before you use the card for this purpose. Cash advances can be a *very* expensive way to get money.

payments and purchases is unimportant, since only the final balance is used to calculate the finance charge.

Cardholder Freebies

Many card companies offer a variety of free benefits to attract and keep cardholders. The benefits vary from one card company to the next and sometimes among different cards issued by the same financial institution. Issuers sometimes require that you qualify for a premium card (sometimes at a higher annual fee) to receive the extra benefits. Whether the benefits offered by a card company hold much value for you depends on your own particular needs. You may find that a few of the added benefits offered by a card company are actually quite useful while other benefits have little value. If you are unlikely to use any of the extra services, you may be able to find cards that have fewer bells and whistles but offer lower interest rates and/or annual fees.

Purchase protection. This reimburses you in case something purchased with the card is stolen, lost, or damaged within ninety days of the purchase date. If you use your credit card to purchase a new lamp that falls to the floor and breaks when you carry it into the house, your purchase price will be refunded. This benefit was once quite popular but is now being discontinued by many card companies.

Extended warranties. Extended warranties double the manufacturer's warranty for up to one additional year. Thus, if the manufacturer provides a ninety-day warranty, the credit card company will give you an extra ninety days of warranty protection. If the regular warranty is for two years, you will receive an extra year of warranty protection (for a total of three years) from the credit card company. An extended warranty for no additional cost is a valuable benefit.

Collision insurance damage waiver protection. Some credit card companies provide rental car collision insurance so that you can decline the costly collision insurance coverage offered by the rental car company. Paying for a rental car with a credit card that includes collision insurance allows you to sign a waiver and decline the rental company's coverage. Collision insurance from credit card companies is secondary to the coverage of your own automobile insurance policy. This is a valuable benefit if you occasionally rent automobiles and your regular insurance doesn't cover damage to a rental vehicle.

Emergency assistance. Certain credit card companies provide cardholders with emergency medical and legal assistance and emergency cash. Emergency assistance mainly benefits individuals who do a lot of traveling and are likely to end up in a place where they don't know anyone and can't speak the local language.

Travel clubs. Some credit card companies allow cardholders to earn a rebate when travel is booked through an affiliated travel agency. Rebates of 5 percent are generally restricted to the amounts a cardholder spends for lodging and transportation. Payments for travel must generally be made with the appropriate credit card in order to qualify for

If you are a good money manager who pays the full amount charged on your credit card account each month, choose a card from an issuer that does not charge an annual fee. Credit card issuers that do not charge an annual fee often charge a high interest rate.

Figure 25

FREQUENT FLIER AFFINITY CARDS

Most major airlines have an exclusive agreement with a financial institution to issue a special credit card that allows cardholders to charge purchases and earn frequent flier credits. These credits can be accumulated and added to the credits a cardholder earns from flying on an airline to earn free trips or seating upgrades. In general, each dollar charged (cash advances don't count) translates into one frequent flier mile. A cardholder who averages monthly charges of $800 would earn 800 frequent flier credits each month, or 9,600 credits each year. Some airlines award a free round-trip ticket for 20,000 credits, allowing this cardholder to accumulate nearly enough credits to earn a free round-trip airline ticket every other year. Not a bad deal if the card company charges a reasonable annual fee. An individual with a job that involves extensive travel has the potential to earn enough credits for several free flights each year.

Some larger airlines and their affinity cards include the following:

Airline/Phone	Card Issuer	The Deal
American Airlines (800) 882–8880	Citibank Visa or MasterCard	One credit per dollar charged
Continental Airlines (800) 525–0280	Midland Bank Visa or MasterCard	One credit per dollar charged
Delta Airlines (800) 221–1212	Diners Club	One credit per two dollars charged
TWA (800) 221–2000	Getaway Card	One credit per dollar charged
United Airlines (800) 421–4655	First Card Visa or MasterCard	One credit per dollar charged
USAir (800) 872–4322	NationsBank Visa	One credit per dollar charged

a rebate. Membership in a travel club can be a valuable benefit if you do a lot of traveling. Travel clubs sometimes also offer discounts on special travel packages.

Affiliation benefits. Some financial institutions have an arrangement whereby a particular organization is rewarded for your use of a special credit card. For example, you may be solicited by a credit card issuer that agrees to donate a few cents to your college alma mater each time you use the card to pay for a purchase. Likewise, you might choose a card that is affiliated with an environmental organization of which you are a member. An increasingly popular affiliation card allows you to earn airline frequent flier credits (i.e., credits that reward you with free airline trips or seating upgrades) when you charge purchases on a particular credit card. Affiliation cards generally have a relatively high annual fee, a high interest rate, or both. You may notice that advertisements for affiliation cards seldom mention the meager amount that affiliated organizations receive from the use of these cards. Don't ask why.

CHAPTER 7

Automobile Loans

Automobile loan payments consume a large portion of the incomes earned by many individuals and families. Payments on automobile loans are a fact of life for many people, from the time they are old enough to drive to the time they are too old to drive. Rising automobile prices have been accompanied by equally large increases in the monthly payments required to finance the purchase of these cars. High monthly payments on automobile loans have caused manufacturers and dealers to promote longer-term loans and leasing as alternatives to familiar thirty-six- and forty-eight-month loans. Long used by businesses, leases, compared with borrowing and buying, have both advantages and disadvantages. Some individuals actually still pay cash for their automobiles!

Vehicle loans are a major source of revenues and profits for many lenders. Banks, savings & loans, credit unions, finance companies, and vehicle dealers and manufacturers have all been attracted to the automobile credit business. Automobiles serve as desirable collateral even though vehicles are mobile and occasionally disappear. An active secondary market in used vehicles allows lenders to easily dispose of automobiles and trucks in the event a borrower fails to make required loan payments. Lending experience and regularly published data allow lenders to accurately estimate the fair market value of the vehicles both when they are first purchased and over their useful lives. Knowing the value of collateral helps a lender determine how much money can safely be loaned.

The short maturities of most vehicle loans are an attraction for many lenders that want their money returned relatively quickly. Short- and intermediate-term loans help protect a lender from the numerous things that can go wrong over long periods of time, and they allow the lender to more accurately forecast factors that affect a loan's profitability and risk. Market rates of interest (which affect the lender's cost of funds), inflation (which affects the purchasing power of the loan payments), and the market value of collateral are all important considerations for lenders.

Short- and intermediate-term loans are also desirable because of a reduced likelihood that there will be a deterioration in a borrower's ability to service his or her debts. The longer the time until a loan is to be repaid the greater the chance there will be a decline in a borrower's financial strength and cash flow (e.g., the borrower divorces, becomes seriously ill, or loses his or her job). Changes in a borrower's financial status can occur over the short term, of

Figure 26

AUTOMOBILE INSTALLMENT CREDIT, 1970–92

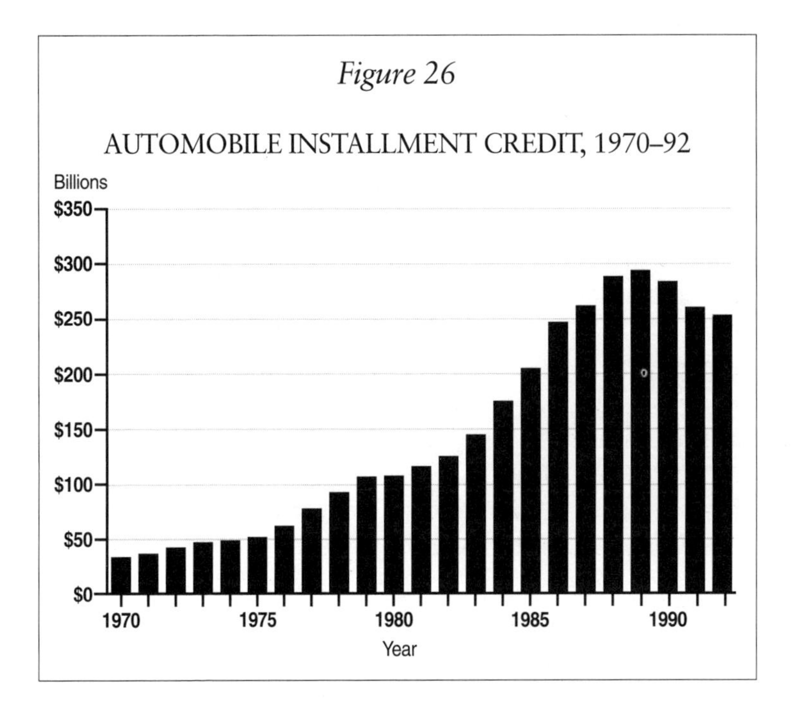

course, but major changes are less likely than for periods of many years.

Characteristics of Automobile Loans

Automobile loans nearly always stipulate monthly payments for a period of three, four, or five years, depending on the term that is offered by the lender and chosen by the borrower. Some lenders refuse to make five-year loans. Required payments on an automobile loan may be constant or adjustable, depending on whether the loan is made at a fixed interest rate or a variable interest rate. The lender retains the title to the car during the term of the loan to make certain that the vehicle being used as collateral cannot be sold by the borrower before the loan is fully repaid. The title is eventually turned over to the borrower when the final loan payment is made.

A borrower who falls behind in making the required loan payments runs the risk that the lender will take possession and sell the car. It is not unknown for lenders to dispatch employees (recovery specialists) in the dark of night to recover vehicles from delinquent borrowers. This is dangerous work! The recovered cars are then offered for sale to individual buyers or through wholesale auctions. Most lenders do not want to have to repossess a car on which they are likely to lose money. Thus, if there is a reasonable chance a loan can be salvaged, lenders will often go out of their way to work with a borrower who has fallen behind on a loan obligation. On the other hand, lenders don't want to be placed in a position of having their collateral fall in value at the same time that interest is accumulating on an overdue loan. A borrower remains responsible for any part of the outstanding loan balance that remains after a repossessed vehicle is sold. The lender is obligated to return to the borrower any proceeds from the disposal that exceed the balance remaining on the loan.

The Amount That Can Be Borrowed

Lenders prefer to structure a loan (i.e., establish the down payment, loan length, and payment size) so as to ensure that the market value of the collateral is greater than the outstanding balance on the loan. Because automobiles normally experience a steep decline in value during the first several years of ownership, most lenders are reluctant to lend the entire purchase price to a buyer. It is not unusual for a lender to lend a maximum of 80 to 90 percent of an automobile's purchase price, although the percentage sometimes goes as high as 100 percent. One hundred percent financing means that a car buyer is able to borrow the entire purchase price. The larger the proportion of the purchase price a lender is willing to finance, the more money the lender stands to lose in the event it becomes necessary to repossess and sell the vehicle. Lenders that have low down payment requirements tend to attract the borrowers that are most likely to default on a loan.

The larger the proportion of a vehicle's purchase price you borrow, the more finance charges you will have to pay over the life of the loan. An $18,000 loan requires 50 percent more in finance charges than a $12,000 loan that has the same interest rate and term. Choosing to borrow a smaller proportion of an automobile's purchase price may allow you to negotiate for a slightly lower interest rate because of the improved position of the lender who is less likely to suffer a loss on the loan. An added advantage of making a large down payment is that you will be unable to fritter away your savings on something else, since the savings will be tied up in the automobile.

If you are having difficulty making loan payments, you may want to consider contacting the Consumer Credit Counseling Service, a nonprofit organization that attempts to arrange a payment plan that is acceptable to you and your creditors. To locate the office nearest you, call (800) 388–2227 or write National Foundation for Consumer Credit, 8611 Second Avenue, Suite 100, Silver Spring, MD 20910.

Length of a Loan

Most automobile loans are for terms of three, four, or five years, although some lenders now go as long as six years while other lenders forgo even five-year loans. The length of automobile loans has crept upward as lenders have sought to keep monthly payments within the reach of more families. It is not necessarily in a lender's interest to make five- and six-year loans, because the longer term increases the likelihood that the outstanding balance on a loan will exceed the market value of the vehicle being used as collateral. This places the lender in an unfavorable position if it is necessary to repossess and sell a vehicle being used as collateral.

Unfortunately, relentless price increases for new and used automobiles have resulted in fewer and fewer people being able to afford the payments required on three-year loans. Paying $222 per month for three years to buy a $7,000 car is one thing. Paying $508 per month to buy a $16,000 automobile is another story, especially considering that the payments must come from your *after-tax* income. Rather than reduce the size of the payments by lowering the interest rates they charged (not likely!), lenders achieved the same result by lengthening the term of the loans, which, in turn, increased the number of payments required of borrowers. Lengthening the $16,000 loan from three years to five years decreases the monthly payment from $508 to $322.

To save on interest charges, you should choose a loan with a short maturity so long as you are confident you will be able to handle the payments. Figure 27 shows the difference in interest charges for loans with different maturity lengths. The $17,000 loan used in the example has total interest charges of $3,682 when a five-year loan is chosen. In-

Figure 27

PAYMENTS AND FINANCE CHARGES FOR AUTOMOBILE LOANS OF DIFFERENT LENGTHS

Loan length	3 years	4 years	5 years
Amount borrowed	$17,000	$17,000	$17,000
Interest rate	8%	8%	8%
Monthly payment	$532.72	$415.02	$344.70
Total payments	$19,177.92	$19,920.96	$20,682.00
Total interest paid	$2,177.92	$2,920.96	$3,682.00

terest charges fall by nearly $1,500 to $2,178 if a three-year payoff is selected.

Interest Rates on Automobile Loans

Although interest rates charged on new automobile loans change relatively slowly, they do fluctuate in sympathy with changes in market rates of interest on other types of credit instruments. Interest rates on Treasury securities and corporate bonds, the prime rate charged for short-term loans to creditworthy customers, and rates on mortgage loans all affect the interest rates that financial institutions charge on automobile loans. If expectations for increased inflation or a tightened credit availability cause an increase in market interest rates, the interest rates charged by lenders on automobile loans will also increase.

The interest rate charged on automobile loans is affected by market interest rates because market rates affect how much a lender must pay to attract money from savers and how much can be earned by making other types of loans. The higher the rate a financial institution must pay to savers, the higher the rate the institution will attempt to charge on the loans that it makes. Falling interest rates cause a decline in a financial institution's cost of money that is likely to result in a reduction in the rate the institution charges on automobile loans. A decision to change the interest rates charged on these loans will also depend on the actions of competing lenders.

How the Interest Rate Affects Your Payment

A higher interest rate charged on an automobile loan of a given size and length results in larger monthly payments. Suppose you decide to purchase a new $18,000 car and require a $14,000 loan to supplement your $4,000 down payment. If you choose a four-year loan at an annual rate of 7 percent the monthly payment will be $335.25. The same loan made at a 10 percent interest rate will require monthly payments of $355.08, an increase of approximately $20. The small increase in monthly payments caused by a relatively large increase in interest rates results from the short-term nature of the loan. Payments on a short-term loan go mostly to reducing the outstanding balance rather than to paying interest charges. On the 7 percent loan, the initial $335.35 payment is allocated $81.67 to paying interest and

> The Federal Trade Commission advises consumers to beware of companies that promise to fix your credit history or clean up your credit report.

$253.68 to reducing the principal. Subsequent $335.35 payments will be increasingly allocated to reducing the principal. By comparison, the initial $355.08 payment on the 10 percent loan will go $116.67 to interest and $238.41 to principal reduction.

The nominal change in payment size that results from a relatively large change in the interest rate is one reason that consumer borrowing for automobile purchases is not greatly affected by interest rate changes. Consumers considering an automobile loan tend to be influenced more by the size of the payments they will be required to make than by the interest rate they will be charged. As an informed borrower, however, you should be aware that even a relatively small payment increase can amount to a substantial amount of money over time. For example, the 10 percent loan noted above will result in nearly $1,000 in extra interest charges over the four-year life of the loan, as compared with the same loan at 7 percent interest. The additional cumulative finance charges caused by a higher interest rate is even greater for a five-year loan.

Fixed versus Variable Interest Rates

Some, but not all, lenders offer automobile loans at both fixed and variable interest rates. A loan with a fixed interest rate locks you into a constant monthly payment for the life of the loan, while a loan with a variable interest rate involves adjustments in both the interest rate and the payments at scheduled intervals, usually annually or semiannually. Constant payments have the advantage of being easier to budget because you know exactly how much money must be paid each month. An adjustable rate loan is more difficult to budget (although this type of loan typically includes limits on the amounts by which interest rates and payments can be increased), but it may have the advantage of smaller overall finance charges. Choosing between fixed-rate and variable-rate loans depends on the initial interest rate difference and your expectations regarding interest rates over the next several years. If you expect rising rates you should generally choose a fixed-rate loan.

Refinancing Automobile Loans

A significant decline in market interest rates after you have made a commitment on a fixed-rate loan may make it worthwhile to look into refinancing your loan. Refinancing means that you use the proceeds of a new loan to pay off the balance on an existing loan. Refinancing provides an opportunity to reduce the interest cost of financing your car when interest rates have fallen enough that interest savings will more than offset the trouble and fees of making a new loan. Refinancing mortgages has long been a popular activity of homeowners, who stand to save substantial interest charges on large loans with long terms. Automobile loan refinancings offer more modest savings and are generally feasible only in the early stages of a loan. Still, if interest rates fall several percentage points within the first year of your loan, you may find that you can refinance and lower your monthly payments by $20 or so. If you are thinking about refinancing, make certain that you will not end up paying substantial fees to the lender. Also make sure that reduced payments on the new loan will not primarily ensue from a loan extension (you are required to make more payments) rather than a lower interest rate.

Leasing as an Alternative to Borrowing and Buying

Auto analysts estimate that nearly 25 percent of all new auto sales are being financed with leases. Automobile dealers increasingly choose to advertise lease payments rather than loan payments and/or vehicle prices, and no wonder! Dealers have found that customers who lease a vehicle have greater dealer loyalty than customers who purchase a vehicle. Even more important, a lease appears to be a very inexpensive method of obtaining the use of a vehicle compared with the loan payments that would be required to finance the purchase of the vehicle. The payment difference between leasing and borrowing is especially noticeable for luxury vehicles that cost $25,000 and above. Are the advertised lease payments too good to be true? Perhaps.

Who Owns the Vehicle When the Payments End?

Lease payments are indeed lower than the corresponding loan payments that would be required to purchase the same vehicle. Most current leases, however, leave ownership of the leased vehicle with the lessor (the financial institution that owns the vehicle and receives the lease payments) rather than the lessee (the party that uses the vehicle and makes the lease payments) at the termination of the lease. This type of lease requires two to four years of monthly

> To locate a credit bureau, check the Yellow Pages under *Credit Bureaus* or *Credit Reporting Agencies.* If several are listed, call to determine which bureaus maintain your file.

payments (the number depends on the terms of the lease), and it generally permits but does not require you to *purchase* the car from the lessor at the end of the lease at a price stipulated in the lease. Although the payments on a loan used to finance a vehicle purchase are typically higher than comparable lease payments, a loan allows you to remain the owner of the vehicle following your last payment.

The distinction of who owns the vehicle at the end of the required payments is the major reason for the differences between loan payments and lease payments. A lease payment is largely a function of the expected decline in the market value of the vehicle (i.e., the *depreciation)* during the term of the lease. A car that is expected to retain an unusually large portion of its original purchase price should have a relatively low lease payment because the lessor will retain possession of a car that can be sold at a favorable price at the termination of the lease. By contrast, a vehicle that typically loses a large portion of its market value in the first few years of ownership is likely to have relatively large lease payments to compensate the lessor for this expected loss in value.

Who Should Lease?

Most leases are convenient, ongoing financial arrangements whereby you sign a two-, three-, or four-year lease, drive the vehicle for the allotted time, return the vehicle to the lessor at the termination of the lease, and repeat the process with a new car and a new lease. Leasing doesn't allow you to build any equity (ownership value) in a vehicle; at the same time, it does free you from worry about both depreciation and trading vehicles. Depreciation, the major expense of owning

Figure 28

OPEN- VERSUS CLOSED-END LEASES

Financial institutions write two types of leases on automobiles. The two leases differ with regard to ownership of the vehicle at the termination of the lease and the responsibility for more rapid than expected depreciation in the market value of the leased vehicle during the term of the lease.

Open-end lease An open-end lease holds you, the lessee, responsible for any difference between the projected residual value of the vehicle and the actual market value at the end of the lease period. The projected value of the leased vehicle will be included in the lease agreement you sign. If a leased car depreciates faster than anticipated, you will be required to pay the difference between the expected value and the market value at the termination of the lease. Suppose a monthly lease payment is based on the assumption that a vehicle will have a $6,000 resale value at the end of the lease. If the market value turns out to be only $4,000, you will be required to come up with the $2,000 difference if you have entered into an open-end lease. Abuses and consumer misunderstandings and complaints caused Congress to pass legislation in the late 1970s limiting the amount a lessee is required to pay on an open-end lease. Open-end leases continue to be offered, although they have mostly been replaced with closed-end leases.

Closed-end lease A closed-end lease (sometimes called a *walkaway lease)* specifies the price at which a lessee *may* purchase a vehicle at the end of the lease. No purchase is required of a lessee, who can walk away from the vehicle and enter into a lease for a new vehicle. A closed-end lease shifts the risk of overestimating the residual value of a leased vehicle to the lessor, who agrees to absorb losses that stem from rapid depreciation. A closed-end lease frees you from worry about being required to come up with additional funds at the termination of the lease to pay for unanticipated depreciation in the leased vehicle. A closed-end lease *does* hold you responsible for above-normal wear or mileage.

a newer model car, is the concern of the lessor, not the lessee, although the lease payment will be set at a level that compensates the lessor for expected depreciation.

A lease is most appropriate if you regularly trade for a new car every two or three years. Leasing allows you to move from one vehicle to another without being required to negotiate a trade or come up with a large down payment. On the other hand, if you ordinarily keep a car for six or seven years, your best bet is probably to finance the purchase with a loan (or with savings). Financing the car with a three-year loan will allow you to drive the vehicle an additional three or four years free of loan payments. The reprieve from $300 or $400 in monthly car payments provides breathing room to take care of other financial matters, such as adding savings to a retirement fund or paying off other loans. Owning is likely to be especially advantageous if you take very good care of your car and you don't drive a lot of miles. Your car should last longer and have added value when you decide to trade.

Some Important Things You Should Know about Leasing

A lease is an alternative method of acquiring the use of a vehicle. Don't make the mistake of moving up to a more expensive automobile just because the lower lease payment

> Hefty financing costs are only one of several expenses associated with owning a new automobile. You are also likely to encounter increased taxes and insurance, along with substantially higher depreciation compared with depreciation on your previous car.

Figure 29

A NEW WRINKLE IN AUTOMOBILE LEASES

As leases gained consumer acceptance and began capturing a substantial share of the market for automobile financing, manufacturers and financial institutions sought to attract more business by offering leases with new wrinkles. In late 1993 General Motors was offering three different lease plans, one of which required a single large payment at the beginning of the lease. One unusual product offered by Ford Motor Company was a "lifetime" lease that included six successive cars over a period of twelve years. The six consecutive leases for two years each required a constant lease payment for the entire twelve years. Although Ford assumes substantial risk in offering six cars over such a long period at a fixed payment, the company creates loyalty among customers, who make a commitment to the company's products.

(compared with a loan payment) fits into your budget. Remember that you have to start again from scratch at the termination of a lease. In this respect, leasing an automobile is like renting a home: Both involve lower payments than ownership.

The lessor's profit. Lease payments are established to provide a return on the lessor's capital that is tied up in the leased vehicle. The lower the return a lessor will accept, the more you should benefit with lower lease payments.

Qualifying. You must normally have a good credit record to qualify for a lease. A lease with a low down payment places the lessor at greater risk of suffering a substantial loss in the event you default on a lease obligation.

Getting the best deal. You should aggressively shop for a lease just as you would shop among dealers for the best price on a car and among financial institutions for the lowest rate on a loan. Financial institutions will sometimes offer special leasing deals. Likewise, automobile manufacturers will occasionally offer attractive leases on particular models they are promoting.

Breaking a lease. Terminating a lease early will negate all of the calculations regarding residual value and the lessor's expected return. Lessors normally charge a substantial penalty in the event you decide to terminate a lease early. Sign a lease only if you are prepared to fulfill the terms of the lease.

Mileage. Leases typically specify a maximum number of miles you can drive a vehicle without getting hit with an excess-mileage charge. A lease typically allows 15,000 miles annually before an extra charge is imposed. You should attempt to negotiate for a higher allowance when you expect to exceed the mileage allowance.

Maintenance. You are responsible for all the repairs, insurance, service, and maintenance on a leased vehicle. At the completion of the lease, you will be assessed a penalty for excessive wear.

Taxes. Sales taxes, if applicable, are ordinarily added to each lease payment. You are also responsible for paying any other taxes and fees, such as title, license, and registration, related to owning the vehicle.

Down payment. Most automobile leases require a nonrefundable down payment, usually $1,000 or so, depending on the value of the automobile being leased. You may also be required to put up a security deposit (generally refundable). Down payments and security deposits make leases less desirable.

The Best Choice: Paying with Your Savings

Your best bet may be to buy an automobile for cash. Paying cash allows you to avoid the interest charges, fees, and monthly payments of a loan or a lease. It also causes you to have more of your own money invested in the vehicle you purchase.

The choice of whether to use your savings or take out a loan should depend, in part, on the rate of return you are earning on your savings compared with the rate of interest you will be required to pay a lender. As a general rule, you should choose the borrowing route if you can earn a higher after-tax return on your savings than the bank will charge on a loan. If you are unlikely to earn a return that is comparable to the interest rate you will be charged on a car loan, you should use your savings to buy a new automobile.

Suppose your savings are currently earning an annual return of 5 percent and you expect this rate to continue for the next several years. After paying taxes at a rate of 30 percent, you earn an after-tax return of 3.5 percent (the remaining 70 percent of the 5 percent annual return). If lenders are currently charging from 7 to 8 percent annual interest on four-year automobile loans, you are better off financing a car purchase by drawing on your savings rather than by taking out a loan. This assumes, of course, that you have accumulated sufficient savings to pay for the car.

> If you have to take out a five-year car loan to be able to make the payments, you should probably consider purchasing a less costly car that you could pay off in either three or four years.

Figure 30

MONTHLY SAVINGS REQUIRED
TO ACCUMULATE $17,000

Return on Savings	Savings Period 36 Months	48 Months	60 Months
5 percent	$438.67	$320.66	$249.98
6 percent	432.17	314.25	243.66
7 percent	425.74	307.92	237.45
8 percent	419.39	301.69	231.37
9 percent	413.10	295.55	225.39
10 percent	406.88	289.50	219.53

A method for accumulating adequate savings is to regularly set aside a certain amount of money into a fund specifically designated for the purchase of a vehicle. The required contributions into the fund depend on three factors: the return you expect to earn on your savings, the length of time before you intend to purchase the car, and the amount of money you wish to accumulate. The higher the price of the car, the sooner you want to buy the car, and the lower the return you expect to earn, the greater the monthly contribution you must make.

Setting aside adequate savings sounds great, but how can you go about saving money for your next car purchase when you are currently paying for the car you are now driving? This amounts to making double payments. How about driving your present car an additional year or two after paying off the current loan? If you bought your current car two years ago with the proceeds of a three-year loan, bite the bullet and plan to drive the car three more years. During the two years following repayment of the current loan, continue to make the same payments into a savings fund for your next car purchase. Even though you may not be able to accumulate enough in two years to pay the entire cost of a new car, the savings will enable you to make a large down payment that substantially reduces the loan payments required to make your next car purchase. In fact, one more cycle and you should be sufficiently ahead of the game to pay cash for your next purchase.

You should generally avoid the purchase of credit life insurance when you borrow money. Credit life is a better deal for the seller than it is for you.

CHAPTER 8

Home Loans

Houses are so expensive that most families interested in purchasing a home have little choice but to borrow a substantial sum of money. Buying a home with borrowed money requires several important decisions, including how much you can afford to spend, how large a down payment you will make, whether you should choose a loan with a variable or a fixed interest rate, and how long the loan should run. Real estate loans often include points and fees that add many thousands of dollars to the cost. Interest costs over the life of a home loan are quite large and are likely to exceed the amount of money you borrow.

Buying a home is synonymous with borrowing money—big time! A house (or series of houses) is the single most expensive thing you are likely to buy during your lifetime (although you may cumulatively spend more on automobiles), and the loan to finance the purchase will consume a major part of your income for fifteen to twenty-five years or longer. This is serious borrowing! A home loan involves such a large amount of money for so many years that you need to understand all of your options so that you will know what you are doing when you get ready to borrow.

Why Buy a Home?

Most home buyers have several motives that cause them to sink tens of thousands of dollars into a down payment; pay additional thousands of dollars in fees to attorneys, an appraiser, and a lender; and sign a commitment to make monthly payments for the next 200 to 300 months. Mostly, home buyers are looking for a place to live. After all, you have to eat and sleep somewhere, and it may as well be where you are comfortable. Home buyers generally view a home as an investment that will appreciate in value and provide tax benefits. Although this is often a secondary motive for buying a home, the investment aspect plays an important role in determining the style, size, and location of the home that is purchased. Perhaps you want a home that lets others know how financially successful you have become. After all, big wheels generally have big homes.

> Try not to use credit to buy things that will be used up before your loan repayments are complete.

A Home as an Investment

Economists who measure and interpret economic data for the federal government classify home construction as investment spending rather than as consumption. Individuals and families have much the same view of home ownership—a home is not just a place to live but also an investment that should increase in value. Homeowners of today certainly have more modest expectations regarding the appreciation potential of their homes than homeowners of fifteen to twenty years ago when real estate prices were in an inflationary spiral. The market value of a home is affected by a number of factors, including local economic activity, population shifts, and general inflationary pressures.

A home should be considered one component of an investment portfolio that includes savings accounts, stocks, certificates of deposit, the pension maintained by your employer, mutual fund shares, and other investments you may own. The investment characteristics of a home provide a balance to the financial assets that make up the largest part of most individual portfolios. During inflationary times, for example, home values generally increase, whereas financial assets perform poorly.

The Tax Advantages of Home Ownership

A major financial advantage of home ownership is the opportunity for a considerable reduction in federal and state income taxes. A mortgage loan to finance a home purchase can result in thousands of dollars in annual tax savings because of laws that favor home ownership. The tax savings result from using mortgage interest and property tax payments as deductions to reduce your taxable income. Deductions for mortgage interest and property taxes reduce taxable income if, when combined with other itemized deductions (e.g., charitable contributions, state and local income taxes, and certain medical expenses), they cause total itemized deductions to exceed the standard deduction. The tax savings you gain from owning a home also depend on the tax rate applicable to your income. The higher the rate at which your income is taxed, the greater the tax savings you reap from a given deduction.

The interest deduction is limited to the interest portion of your monthly home loan payments. This deduction declines each month as the outstanding balance on your loan is reduced even though the payment to the lender remains the same. Tax savings from a mortgage loan are largest in the early years, when your loan balance is highest and you pay substantial amounts of interest. Interest expenses and the accompanying tax deductions are relatively small in the years just before the loan is scheduled to be retired. Once your mortgage is completely repaid, only annual property taxes are available as an itemized deduction.

How Much Home Can You Afford?

Although newspaper and magazine articles on home buying often include rules of thumb for determining the maximum you should allocate to housing, there are no hard-and-fast rules that apply to everyone. The size of your income is obviously important, as is the amount of funds you have available for a down payment. The stability of your income is another consideration. Committing yourself to an extended series of costly expenditures is a risky proposition when

> You may withhold payment on defective merchandise or services purchased with a credit card, provided that you have made a good-faith effort to return the goods or resolve the problem with the seller.

your current employment and income are uncertain. You must consider other priorities and obligations: emergency funds, health insurance, adequate life insurance, and so forth. The size of your family will play a central part in determining how much of your income is consumed by expenditures on food, transportation, and so forth, and how much will be available for housing.

The interest rate you must pay on a mortgage loan is an important determinant of how expensive a home you can purchase. A high interest rate causes large monthly payments that make it more difficult to service a given amount of debt. Borrowing $90,000 at 7 percent is one thing; borrowing the same amount at 12 percent is something else. The interest rate is of less importance if you have saved enough money to pay cash or make a substantial down payment.

The amount of home you can afford is partly a function of the importance you attach to home ownership. Some families consider owning a nice home to be so important that they are willing to surrender vacations, new cars, expensive clothes, and many of the things that other families consider necessities. Two similar families with identical incomes and assets but different spending priorities can spend significantly different amounts on housing.

Owning a home, especially an older home, requires cash outlays in addition to the monthly loan payments. Home ownership means annual property taxes that may amount

Figure 31

INTERREST RATES AND MORTGAGE PAYMENTS

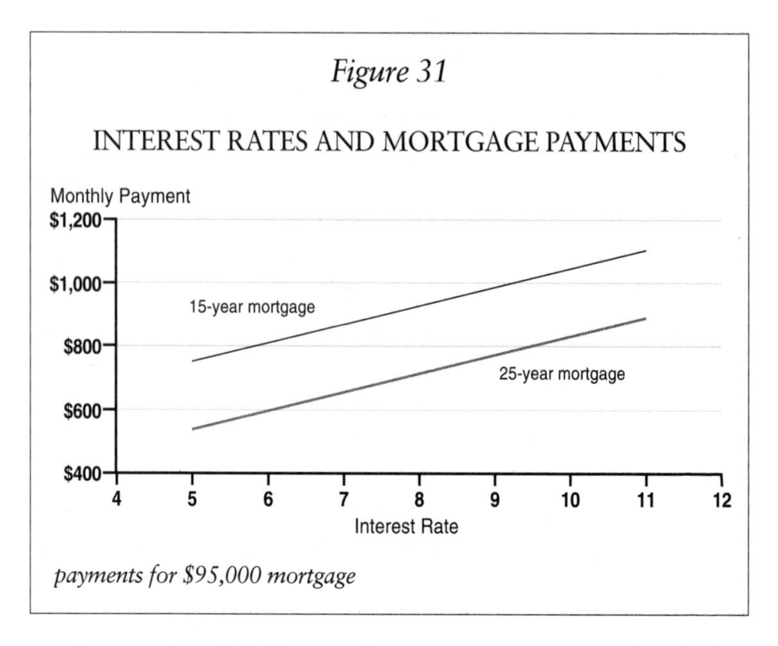

payments for $95,000 mortgage

to thousands of dollars and insurance coverage that is becoming increasingly expensive. Maintenance can be another major expense, especially when a home is more than ten years old. Appliances break, roofs leak, wood needs painting, yards need mowing, carpets need replacing, and the beat goes on. If you currently own a home, you are already coping with these headaches. Maintaining a home in top-notch shape requires physical effort and substantial monetary expenditures.

Importance of the Down Payment

The down payment you are able to make plays a chief role in determining the amount of home you are able to buy and the size of the loan payment you must make. If you are interested in purchasing as expensive a home as possible (perhaps you wish to impress your mother-in-law), a large down payment will allow you to borrow a greater amount of money. Of course, you must be able to service the monthly loan payment. On the other hand, if you have already picked out the home you wish to purchase, a large down payment will cause you to borrow less money and allow you to choose a loan with a shorter maturity or smaller payments.

Assuming that you have the funds available to make a large down payment, is this an advisable course of action? When you buy a $100,000 home, should you make the $10,000 minimum down payment required by the lender, or should you plunk down $25,000 or even $35,000? The answer depends, in part, on the return you are able to earn on your funds compared with the interest rate you will be paying on the loan. If you consistently earn an annual return of 12 to 15 percent on your investments at the same time that you can borrow money for a home purchase at 8 percent, you should put down as little as possible so that you can maximize the amount of money you have available for investment. On the other hand, if you are a conservative investor who keeps a large proportion of your wealth in money market funds or Treasury bills, you are unlikely to

> It is worthwhile to shop extra hard when you are in the market for a home mortgage. Borrowing to buy a home ordinarily involves such a large amount of money that a reduction of an extra eighth of one percent can produce substantial interest savings over the life of a twenty-year loan.

Figure 32

HOW THE SIZE OF A DOWN PAYMENT AFFECTS MONTHLY PAYMENTS AND INTEREST EXPENSE

The size of the down payment you make on a home has a major impact on the size of the monthly payments you will be required to make. It also affects the total amount of interest you will pay over the life of the loan.

Purchase price of home: $110,000
Term of loan: 25 years (300 monthly payments)
Interest rate on loan: 8.25%

Down Payment	Payment	Total Payments	Total Interest
$10,000	$805.23	$241,569	$141,569
20,000	724.71	217,413	127,413
30,000	644.19	193,257	113,413
40,000	563.66	169,098	99,098
50,000	483.14	144,942	84,942

earn a return on your investments that exceeds the interest rate you have will to pay on a home loan, and you should favor making a substantial down payment to reduce your interest expense.

If you choose to make a large down payment, don't drain all your financial resources. Hold back a portion of your liquid assets to finance an emergency fund. You also want to have funds available to take advantage of particularly good deals that occasionally come your way. Don't make such a large down payment that you leave yourself financially strapped.

Financing the Purchase of a Home

Available financing will play a major role in determining how expensive a home you can purchase. The more restrictive lenders become in granting loans and the higher the interest rate they charge, the less financing you will be able to obtain and afford. If you are actively seeking to purchase a home, contact many lenders regarding the types and costs of loans they are making. You can often get a head start by examining the business section of a local newspaper. Many large newspapers publish a weekly summary of the rates being offered by local financial institutions on both loans and savings instruments. Mortgage loans are frequently available from sources you may overlook. For example, securities brokerage firms and mortgage brokers are likely to be good prospects for mortgage loans. Check the Yellow Pages of your local telephone directory if you are unsure as to whether any of these lenders are located in your community. In fact, you might want to call most or all of the mortgage lenders listed in the Yellow Pages. Just a little better deal can result in substantial savings over the course of twenty to thirty years.

Seller Financing

Sellers are sometimes willing to finance all or a portion of the price of a home, often at a very favorable interest rate. Seller financing is most common when interest rates are high, conventional financing is difficult to obtain, and potential buyers are scarce. A seller might provide supplementary financing for a buyer who is unable to come up with the difference between the selling price and the amount a financial institution will lend. Perhaps you are interested in purchasing a home selling for $80,000. Several lenders have indicated they will lend a maximum of $65,000, meaning that you must come up with $15,000 of your own funds. The seller, however, may be willing to accept $65,000 immediately, along with a note for the remaining $15,000 that is to be repaid in installments over ten years. Depending on how badly a seller wishes to dispose of a home, you may be able to negotiate several financing alternatives.

Conventional Financing

Most lenders offer several types of mortgage loans. The choice you make will affect the size of your payment, the fees you must pay, and the interest rate you are charged.

Conventional loan. The most common type of mortgage loan specifies a fixed interest rate and a constant monthly payment, generally for fifteen, twenty, twenty-five, or thirty years. Financial institutions typically lend a maximum of 75 to 80 percent of a home's appraised value on a conventional loan, meaning that you must come up with a down payment for the remaining 20 to 25 percent. A smaller down payment is required when a borrower chooses to purchase insurance that guarantees the lender against loss. The down payment protects the lender from a loss in the event you are unable or unwilling to keep your end of the bargain to make the monthly mortgage payments in a timely manner. A substantial down payment allows the lender to recover the outstanding balance on the loan even though the home may have to be sold for less than the purchase price.

Fixed monthly payments on a conventional loan are composed partly of interest and partly of principal. If you select a twenty-five- or thirty-year mortgage, payments you make in the early years of the loan will go mostly to interest. Suppose you borrow $90,000 for thirty years at an annual interest rate of 8 percent. The loan requires a $660 monthly payment. The first payment goes to pay $600 in interest (1/12 of 8 percent times $90,000) charged by the lender, and the remaining $60 reduces the outstanding balance on the loan. The next monthly payment covers the second month's interest of $599.59 (1/12 of 8 percent times $89,940) and reduces the loan's principal by $60.41. By the end of the second month, you have made two payments totaling $1,320 and reduced the principal on the loan by only $120.41! Cheer up—at least you're getting a heck of a lot of tax deductions.

FHA-insured loan. Borrowers unable to make the required down payment for a conventional loan may choose to have a loan insured by the Federal Housing Administration (FHA). The FHA has established standards both for homes and for borrowers to qualify for the insurance. A limit is imposed on the amount you can borrow with an FHA-insured loan and also with a VA-insured loan, discussed in the next section. Borrowers who qualify must pay

> Choosing a fifteen-year mortgage over a twenty-five-year mortgage will save you many thousands of dollars in interest charges. The shorter loan is likely to offer a lower interest rate.

the FHA an insurance fee to guarantee that the lender will not suffer a loss in the event the borrower is unable to fulfill the terms of the mortgage loan. FHA-insured loans generally require down payments that range from 3 to 5 percent of the appraised value, the main selling feature for this type of financing.

VA-guaranteed loan. The Veterans Administration (VA) guarantees home loans for veterans of the armed forces. A VA loan guarantees a lender against a loss in the event a home is repossessed and sold for less than the loan's outstanding balance. The guarantee allows lenders to require little or no down payments on these loans. Homes must meet certain construction standards to qualify for a VA loan, and limits are placed on the amount that can be borrowed.

Adjustable-rate mortgage. An adjustable-rate mortgage, or ARM (also called a *variable-rate mortgage),* incorporates a changeable interest rate that is tied to some other interest rate, such as the Treasury bill rate, or to some index of rates, such as the cost of funds index. The rate of interest you are charged on an ARM can change at predetermined intervals (generally, annually or semiannually, as specified in the loan contract) if a change occurs in the associated rate or index. Lenders often prefer to make ARMs because these loans transfer the risk of changing interest rates to borrowers. With a fixed-rate loan you are charged the same interest rate and make the same payment no matter what happens to market interest rates. You know exactly what payments you will be making fifteen years in the future. Lending money at a fixed rate of interest can place the creditor in a bind if interest rates subsequently rise, causing an increase in the lender's cost of funds. A variable-rate loan allows the lender to charge an interest rate that varies with the lender's cost of funds. This is a "no-lose" proposition for a lender.

An ARM will generally offer a lower initial rate of interest than a fixed-rate mortgage, because short-term interest rates (the rates that establish the interest rate charged on an ARM) are generally lower than long-term interest rates. The risk to you is that interest rates will rise after you borrow the money, causing an increase in the rate you are charged on the loan along with a corresponding increase in either the size or the number of payments you must make. ARM loans include limits, called *caps,* on how much interest rates can change during a specific period and over the life of the loan. For example, a loan contract may specify that the interest rate cannot change by more than 2 percent in a given year and cannot change by more than 6 percent over the life of the loan. These caps reduce the risk of taking out an ARM loan. Some ARM loans are, for a fee, convertible into fixed-rate loans, although usually at slightly higher interest rates than available to other borrowers.

Graduated-payment mortgage. A graduated-payment mortgage provides for relatively low mortgage payments in the early years of a loan, to be followed by gradually increasing payments in subsequent years when your income is larger and you are financially able to handle bigger expenses. Payments in the early years of a loan are often lower

> Refinancing a home mortgage often requires fees amounting to thousands of dollars. Be certain the interest savings are worth the fees you are likely to have to pay.

than the interest being charged, causing the outstanding balance of the loan to increase. The monthly payments on a graduated-payment mortgage may be scheduled to increase each year, or at predetermined intervals such as every three years or every five years.

Growing-equity mortgage. This type of mortgage is designed for home buyers who desire to pay off their loan early. Payments are scheduled to increase by a specific amount each month, causing principal to decrease more rapidly than would occur with fixed payments. A growing-equity mortgage can result in repaying a thirty-year loan in fifteen to twenty years, depending on how rapidly payments are scheduled to increase.

Reverse-annuity mortgage. A reverse-annuity mortgage (RAM) allows a homeowner who has no outstanding mortgage to enter into a borrowing agreement whereby the lender provides the homeowner with a series of payments (loans) over a period of years. A RAM is primarily designed to allow a retiree who experiences difficulty meeting living expenses to gradually withdraw the equity in a home. Interest on these loans accumulates so that no payment of interest is required of a borrower. The principal and accumulated interest will eventually be paid in full at the time the home is sold.

Home-equity loan. Home-equity loans have greater similarity to credit card accounts and other types of revolving credit than to mortgage loans. These specialized loans are primarily used by homeowners who seek funds to pay for purchases unrelated to home ownership—a car, a vacation, a new computer. Why is this, you ask? Because the interest you pay on a home-equity loan can be deducted in calculating your federal and state income taxes, while interest paid on credit cards and personal loans cannot. Also, you are likely to obtain a lower interest rate on a home-equity loan compared with what you would pay on most other personal loans, especially credit card accounts. The maximum amount you can borrow on a home-equity loan is generally 70 to 80 percent of the appraised value of the home less the outstanding balance on your first mortgage. Essentially, a home-equity loan allows you to borrow against the equity of your home.

The great danger of a home-equity loan is that you will be tempted to borrow against your home for all kinds of purchases you would not ordinarily make. A home-equity loan allows you to buy more expensive clothes, take longer vacations, and eat out more frequently at nice restaurants. The line of credit created by the home equity loan is accessed by writing checks that immediately add to your loan balance. If you have difficulty controlling your spending, a home-equity loan can cause you to be up to your eyeballs in debt as you head into your retirement years.

Points

Lenders often charge a one-time fee based on a percentage of the amount of the loan. Called *points*, this fee has the effect of increasing the return to the lender and increasing the cost to you. One point is equal to 1 percent of the amount you borrow. If you borrow $85,000 from a lender that charges 7½ percent plus 2 points, you will pay an up-front charge of $1,700 (2 percent of $85,000) that is *in addition to* interest and all other expenses. Points charged on a mortgage loan do not affect the loan's annual percentage rate although they certainly affect the cost of credit to you.

The most points are generally charged on FHA and VA loans as lenders seek compensation for interest rate lids imposed by the government on these particular types of loans. You are likely to find that a lender is willing to negotiate with respect to the interest rate and points that are charged on a loan. For example, a lender may give you the option of choosing a 7½ percent loan with no points, a 7¼ percent loan with 1 point, or a 7 percent loan with 2 points. Your choice between fewer points or a lower interest rate should be primarily influenced by how long you expect to live in the house. If you intend to stay for many years, you are likely to be better off choosing a lower interest rate and paying the points. If you plan to move soon you should generally avoid paying points and accept a higher interest rate. You must consider how much in interest savings a point can buy.

Additional Fees

Home loans generally entail expenses in addition to interest charges. Fortunately, most are one-time expenses charged at the time the loan is finalized. Fees you are likely to be charged at the time you finalize a loan on a home (called the *closing*) include a loan application fee, a loan origination fee, a credit report, an appraisal fee, a real estate transfer

When you make major credit card purchases a day or two following the closing date on your billing cycle you will normally have from fifty to fifty-five days before you are required to pay for these purchases.

tax, a notary fee, a survey fee, a title search, a portion of the year's real estate taxes, and an attorney fee. Is this depressing, or what? Excluding points you will probably be required to pay, these additional expenses may amount to from 3 to 5 percent of the purchase price of the home.

Refinancing

You may find that reduced interest rates available on home loans have made it worthwhile to consider refinancing your old loan. Refinancing involves taking out a new loan and using all or part of the proceeds to pay off the balance on the old loan. Your goal is to reduce the cost of living in your home by reducing the monthly interest you must pay. In fact, you may decide to extend the term of your mortgage by taking out a new loan that has a longer term than your existing mortgage. On the other hand, you may decide to shorten the maturity of the new loan compared with that of your original loan. A lower interest rate will allow you to continue making the same payment as on the old loan while paying off the loan at an earlier date.

The drawback to refinancing is the points and fees you are likely to be charged by the lender. You will probably have to pay several thousand dollars in up-front costs. You will again have to pay points, a loan origination fee, notary fees, and so forth. These fees must be paid even though it may not have been long since you last paid the exact same fees! To determine if it is worthwhile to refinance, follow these steps:

1. Estimate the total fees and points you will have to pay. A lender will be able to provide this information.

Figure 33

THE COSTS OF REFINANCING

Refinancing costs may vary significantly from lender to lender and from region to region. The following ranges of costs are estimates of what you are likely to encounter. The lender that holds your current mortgage may be willing to forgo some of these fees, especially if your existing loan is relatively new.

Application fee	$ 75	to	$300
Appraisal fee	150		400
Survey costs	125		300
Lender's attorney fees	75		200
Title search/insurance	450		600
Home inspection fee	175		350
Loan origination fee	1% of loan amount		
Points	1% to 3% of loan amount		

2. Determine the payment reduction that results from the lower interest rate.
3. Multiply your (income) tax rate by the payment reduction calculated in step 2. Subtract this amount from the payment reduction calculated in step 2. This subtraction adjusts for the reduction in tax deductions caused by a lower interest expense.
4. Calculate how long it will take to recover the closing costs by dividing the after-tax reduction in payments from step 3 into the closing costs determined in step 1.

Suppose you have an $80,000 mortgage that has twenty years remaining until it is paid off. Your top income is taxed at a rate of 33 percent. The loan has a 9 percent interest rate and requires monthly payments of $671. Interest rates have declined in the five years since you obtained the current loan, and a loan officer at the local financial institution indicates you can refinance your existing loan at the current market rate of 7 percent. The loan officer estimates that points and fees will amount to $3,200 and that the monthly payment on your new loan will be $620. The total time required to recover the costs of refinancing is $3,200 divided by the difference in payments ($671 – $620 = $51) minus .33 times the difference in payments, or ninety-four months.

The less time it requires to recover the points and fees you must pay to obtain a new loan, the greater your savings from refinancing. In general, you should consider refinancing a mortgage when you can recover all the costs within three or four years. You should not refinance when the period required to recover the refinancing fees, exceeds the time you plan to live in the home. If you are fortunate enough to locate a lender who will refinance your loan without charging any points or fees you should refinance as frequently as you are able to obtain an interest rate lower than the rate on your current loan.

Glossary

Acceleration clause A loan provision that allows a creditor to demand payment in full when a borrower fails to satisfy the terms of a loan agreement.

Add-on clause A loan provision that allows new purchases to be added to an existing loan agreement.

Adjustable-rate loan (ARM) A loan on which the applicable interest rate fluctuates according to another interest rate or index of interest rates. Also called a *variable-rate loan.*

Annual percentage rate (APR) The cost of credit, expressed as an annual percentage of the amount owed. A standardized method of calculation makes the APR useful in comparing the interest cost of different loans.

Average daily balance The sum of the outstanding credit card balances owed each day during the billing period divided by the number of days in the period.

Balloon clause A clause in a loan agreement that requires a final payment substantially larger than previous payments.

Bankruptcy A legal proceeding whereby a person unable to pay his or her debts in full may be discharged from the obligation to do so.

Billing date On a credit card account, the last date of each month's statement on which transactions are reported.

Cash advance Cash obtained by a charge to a charge card or debit card.

Cash value The savings in a life insurance policy that can be borrowed by the policyholder.

Closed-end credit A one-time loan with specified payments and a predetermined maturity.

Closing costs Costs paid at settlement on a mortgage loan that include discount points, title insurance, escrow fees, attorney fees, recording fees, appraisal fees, notary fees, and so forth.

Collateral Assets pledged as security for a loan.

Compound interest Interest calculated on interest from previous periods as well as on principal.

Conditional sales contract A loan agreement in which title to the underlying property does not pass to the buyer until the last installment payment is made.

Consumer Credit Counseling Service A nonprofit organization that provides credit counseling services for individuals and families with serious financial problems.

Conversion Changing an adjustable-rate mortgage to a fixed-rate mortgage.

Cosigner A person who agrees to keep a loan current if the borrower does not.

Credit agreement A contract between a borrower and a lender.

Credit bureau A private business that gathers and distributes information regarding credit histories of consumers.

Credit history A person's credit record.

Credit insurance Life insurance that repays your loan in the event of your death or disability.

Creditor A person or business that lends money.

Credit rating A creditor's judgment regarding the likelihood you will meet your credit obligations in a timely manner.

Credit risk The possibility a loan will not be fully repaid.

Credit scoring A mathematical method for measuring someone's credit rating according to established relationships.

Debit card A plastic card that allows you to pay for purchases with funds that are immediately transferred from a financial account.

Debt consolidation Replacing several smaller loans that have different maturities and interest rates with a single large loan, generally one that has a longer maturity.

Default Failure to live up to the terms of a contract.

Discount loan A loan on which the total amount of the finance charge is deducted in advance.

Down payment The initial payment on a credit purchase. The down payment reduces a borrower's finance charges and protects a lender's position in the event the borrower defaults.

Due date The date on which a loan payment is due.

Equal Credit Opportunity Act A federal act that bans discrimination in the extension of credit on the basis of age, color, sex, marital status, or race.

Escrow A reserve account to take care of your real estate taxes and home insurance premiums when they come due.

Fair Credit Billing Act A federal act that establishes procedures for correcting billing mistakes, refusing to make payments on defective goods, and promptly crediting payments.

Fair Credit Reporting Act A federal act that regulates the use of credit reports.

Finance charge The total dollar amount you pay to use credit. The finance charge includes interest, service and transaction fees, premiums paid for credit life insurance, and so forth.

Fixed interest rate A constant interest rate charged on a loan.

Grace period On a credit statement, the number of days between the billing date and the due date.

Inflation A general increase in the price level of goods and services.

Installment loan A loan with equal periodic payments

Interest A periodic charge for the use of credit.

Lien The legal right of a creditor to hold or sell property for payment of a claim.

Line of credit The maximum amount of credit a lender will extend to a borrower during a specified period of time.

Loan origination fee A lender's charge for evaluating and preparing a loan. Generally applied to a mortgage loan.

Loan qualification Determining whether you can handle the required payments on a loan.

Lock-in A lender's guarantee concerning the interest rate and fees on a loan.

Margin account A brokerage account that allows the account holder to purchase securities on credit. A margin account can also be used to borrow against securities held in the account.

Maturity date The date on which a loan is to be fully repaid.

Minimum payment The minimum amount that you must pay (usually monthly) on your account.

Mortgage loan A loan to purchase real estate that serves as collateral.

Negative amortization An increase in the outstanding balance on a loan because payments made by the borrower are less than periodic interest charges.

Net worth The difference between the value of assets that are owned and the debts that are owed.

Note A written promise to pay a specific amount of money on a certain date.

Open-end credit A loan agreement in which credit is continuously granted to a predetermined maximum and the borrower is billed periodically to make partial or full payment.

Outstanding Remaining to be paid.

Periodic rate The interest rate charged on a loan during a particular period of time, often monthly.

Prepayment fee The lender's charge for an early payoff of a loan.

Prime rate The interest rate commercial banks charge their most creditworthy customers. The prime rate influences the interest rate charged on consumer loans.

Principal The balance of a debt, excluding interest.

Refinance Revise a loan's payment schedule to extend payments or reduce interest.

Repossession Surrender of an asset by a borrower who has failed to live up to the terms of a loan agreement.

Rule of 78s A mathematical formula to determine how much interest you have paid on a loan at any point in time.

Second mortgage A real estate loan over and above another loan that uses the same real estate as collateral.

Secured credit card A credit card secured by funds deposited in a financial institution.

Secured note A note that includes the pledge of an asset that can be claimed by the creditor in case the borrower fails to meet the terms of the agreement.

Security interest A lender's control over property.

Simple interest Interest calculated on principal only.

Term The length of time between when a loan agreement is signed and when the loan is completely repaid.

Truth in Lending Act A federal law that requires disclosure of the annual percentage rate and the finance charges on a lending agreement.

Unsecured note A lending agreement in which no specific assets are pledged. The borrower's promise is the only guarantee of repayment.

Usury laws State laws regulating interest rates that can be charged by creditors.

Variable-rate loan See *adjustable-rate loan.*

Index

Index